AMERICAN TANK DEVELOPMENT DURING THE COLD WAR

The United States, it's fair to say, was not among the pioneers of tank warfare in the early twentieth century. The M1917, the first US tank, a licence-built copy of the French Renault FT, was introduced too late to take part in World War I and by 1939 the Army had only developed the inadequate M1 Combat Car and M2 Light Tank for service. It was not until July 1940 that the Armor Branch of the US Army was formally created and late in 1941 that a tank – the M3 Lee Medium Tank – entered service that was a match for those of the Axis Powers. Some 6,200 were produced up to 1942 and they saw action in North Africa, on the Eastern Front and in the Pacific with the Americans and their allies.

The outbreak of war in December 1941 mobilised America's industrial might to produce weaponry on a hitherto unimagined scale. In February 1942 production began of the M4 Sherman, one of the most iconic tanks of all time. The Sherman tank, of which some 49,200 were built between 1942 and the end of the War, was one of the most important weapons of World War II, serving in all theatres of war. It also served as a potent symbol of American military and industrial power. While it may have been inferior to the German Panzer IV, Panther and Tiger tanks, the sheer number of Sherman tanks in the American and Allied armies prevailed. The experience of the M4 Sherman against the heavier German tanks, however, showed the need for a heavier and more powerful tank. This led to the development of the M26 Pershing. Armed with an M3 90mm gun, it was the only US tank that could engage the German Pz.Kpfw V Panther or Pz.Kpfw VI Tiger and King Tiger on anything like equal terms. Eventually 2,222 were produced, but only twenty were delivered and saw action in Europe before the end of World War II.

The M3 gun was chosen as the main armament of the first American tank of the Cold War period, the M46 Patton. The M3 was capable of defeating the Soviet-built T-34/85 at any range and the M26 and newer M46 were the US Army's and Marine Corps' most important weapon during the Korean War. The experience of the Korean War and the hotting up of the arms race with the Soviet Union led to the development of a new generation of American medium tanks. The M47 combined the turret of the M42 Medium Tank with the hull of the M46, but this was essentially a stopgap as the US Army developed and introduced its new tank, the M48 Patton. The M47 entered production in 1951 and over 9,000 were built before manufacture ended in November 1953.

The M48 was the iconic American tank of the early Cold War period, serving alongside the M47 in both the United States and in Germany during the 1950s and 60s. The M48 introduced some important new features. Its hull and turret were complete single castings and the design carefully eliminated the shot traps that had plagued previous medium tanks. The driver sat in a central position in the hull front, while the gun was still the old M3, albeit now with an improved muzzle

The M48, armed with the 90mm cannon with its distinctive T-shaped muzzle brake. The M48 was the US Army's Main Battle Tank through the 1950s through into the Vietnam War. (NARA)

Both the M48 and the M60 continued to serve into the 1980s and 90s with National Guard Units. This is an M60A3 of 1-108 Armor, Georgia National Guard, at the National Training Centre, Fort Irwin, CA, in July 1983. (NARA)

brake and ammunition. Over 12,000 M48s were produced before production ceased in 1959 and entered service both in the US Army and the Marine Corps. The M48 went through several variants in its service history, demonstrating the American resolve to develop and evolve existing tank designs, rather than design tanks from scratch. The M48, M48A1 and M48A2 all had Continental AVSI-1790-6 gasoline

An M60A3 TTS of 1st Cavalry Division is ferried across the River Rhine during Exercise Autumn Forge, part of REFORGER 1983, the annual series of field exercises by US and NATO forces in West Germany. (NARA)

An M60A3 TTS (Tank Thermal Site) passes through a German street during Exercise Carbine Fortress 82, part of REFORGER 1983, the annual series of field exercises by US and NATO forces in West Germany. (NARA: SSgt. Bob Simons)

engines, but their powertrain suffered from high fuel consumption and the tanks were inferior in cross country performance to the M47 despite their suspension. In 1963 the US Army began to rebuild its M48 to M48A3 standard, incorporating improved fire-control systems and a AVDS-1790-2 diesel engine. The M48A3 was the principal American tank during the Vietnam War.

As early as 1959 the US Army had decided upon its successor to the M48. The M60 was basically a development of the M48 rather than a new tank. It was armed with the M68 105mm gun, a licence-built version of the Royal Ordnance L7 gun, which was improved to suit US Army requirements. The new tank had an up-gunned M48A2 turret and a new hull design employing cast and welded sections. It was more heavily armoured than the M48 series and had a AVDS-1790-2 diesel engine. It replaced both the M103 Heavy Tank and the M48 series, although the latter was, as we have seen, rebuilt into the M48A3 and later up-gunned as the M48A5. More than 15,000 M60s were built between 1959 and 1983 and it lays claim to the title of the world's first true Main Battle Tank.

In 1961 M60 production switched to the new M60A1. This tank, with over 12,000 produced, had improved ammunition stowage, fire-control systems, suspension and thicker frontal armour. The 1960s saw an attempt by the United States and West Germany to develop a common, new-generation Main Battle Tank, the MBT70. Part of this was the development of the Ford MGM51 Shillelagh Guided Missile Gun system and this was adapted to a special turret designed to be mounted on a standard M60A1 hull in 1964 as the M60A1E1. In 1971 this tank entered service as the M60A2, but the idea to arm MBTs with guided missiles turned out to be a passing fad and its replacement by other new generation anti-tank guided missiles (ATGM) led to the M60A2's withdrawal from service in 1980.

The M60A3, introduced in 1978, was the ultimate version of the M60 and, alongside the M1 Abrams, was the US Army's main battle tank in the early 1980s. The M60A3 finally saw the introduction of a stabilised main gun, as well as new fire controls based on a ballistic computer and a new laser rangefinder. Ironically and thankfully, the M60, like the M1 Abrams, never had the opportunity to prove itself on the battlefields and against the adversary for which it was designed. It was in fact during Operation Desert Storm, the Coalition effort to liberate Kuwait from the forces of Saddam Hussein, that the M60A1 proved its effectiveness in the hands of the United States Marine Corps. That campaign saw the M60 Main Battle Tank, a tank that could trace its lineage back to the end of the World War II, serve alongside a completely new tank and a new concept of armoured warfare.

THE DEVELOPMENT OF THE M1 ABRAMS

As we have seen, the equipment of the US Army and Marine Corps tank force in the 1970s was a direct descendant of the M26 that had been developed at the end of World War II. Efforts to modernise the fleet has begun in the 1960s, but in 1969 Congress cancelled a joint US-German project, the MBT70, in the face of rising costs. Indeed, the cost factor would constrain American tank design throughout the 1970s and beyond and shape the eventual design and capability of the M1 Abrams.

In January 1973 Congress approved the start of the XM1 project, with a brief to design a new Main Battle Tank that could take on and defeat the latest generation of Soviet tanks. It was to be achieved at a unit cost of a little over $507,000 (some 50 per cent more expensive than a single M60A1). One of the major factors in the increased cost was the necessity of having an integrated thermal-imaging nightsight, which accounted for about a quarter of the new tank's total cost. In June of that year Chrysler and General Motors announced that they would both be developing prototypes of the Army's new tank.

In the 1960s the Army had developed a revolutionary tank gas-turbine engine, the AVCO-Lyoming AGT-1500. This was, in essence, a jet engine, funnelling the power through the transmission, and, while it was considerably lighter and simpler than comparative piston engines, it consumed huge amounts of fuel while needing large amount of air drawn into it. While the latter factor was not an issue for helicopters (where these engines had given considerable advantages to the Army's fleet), for ground vehicles it meant that large amounts of dust and dirt were drawn into the engine causing maintenance to be an issue. In the end Chrysler opted for the new gas turbine engine, while General Motors decided on the conventional AVCR-1360 diesel engine for their prototype.

There were other areas of debate and contention for the specifications of the new tank. Principal among these was the main gun. Three contenders had emerged by the mid 1970s: the existing 105mm gun fitted to the M60, the British L7 105mm gun and the German Rheinmetall 120mm gun. While gunnery exercises in 1975 had confirmed the superiority of the larger gun and its suitability to meet future Soviet threats, in the end the 105mm gun was chosen for the XM1 as the T-62 was still considered the mainstay of Warsaw Pact forces at this time. If mobility and firepower are the first two considerations of any successful tank design, then protection is the final factor. Since the 1960s developers at the British Army's research facility at Chobham had been working on a special tank armour which consisted of laminated layers of steel and other material. The 1973 Yom Kippur War had highlighted the vulnerability of conventional tank armour to the shaped warheads fitted to Soviet-made Rocket-Propelled Grenades and anti-tank missiles. The new armour gave much better protection against shaped HEAT (High Explosive Anti-Tank) rounds and was equal to conventional armour in its performance against APFSDS (Armour Piercing Fin-Stabilised Discarding Sabot) rounds. As a result of the experiences of the Yom Kippur War, an American team travelled to the United Kingdom to examine the 'Chobham armour' for themselves and it was decided to consider this new armour, dubbed Burlington by the Americans, for the XM1 design. Other features also added to the protection the crew enjoyed. The bulk of the ammunition, for example, was stored in a rear turret bustle, protected from fire by a blast door, rather than in the main turret or hull as in previous tank designs.

The first two pilot tanks were tested at the Aberdeen Proving Ground in Maryland in the first half of 1976. The new German Leopard 2 was also evaluated at the same time and, while it was considered a better tank, its cost (25 per cent more than either XM1 prototype) proved prohibitive. The first trials came out in favour of the General Motors design, with the significant exception of the AGT-1500 gas turbine engine, the performance of which far exceeded that of its diesel rival. The Army asked both manufacturers to go back to the drawing board with a view to designing a turret capable of accommodating the Rheinmetall 120mm gun, but Chrysler also used this an opportunity to incorporate the new Burlington armour into their prototype. Crucially, they were also able to incorporate other design changes that substantially reduced the unit cost of each tank. As a result, on 12 November 1976, the Army selected the Chrysler design for full-scale engineering-manufacturing development. This involved a pilot of eleven tanks, to be manufactured principally at the Lima Army Tank Plant with secondary production at the Detroit Army Tank Plant. The first pilot tanks were delivered in February 1978 and quickly proved their worth. Indeed, so successful were these initial trials, that on 7 May 1979 the Army placed a low-rate initial production order for 110 tanks.

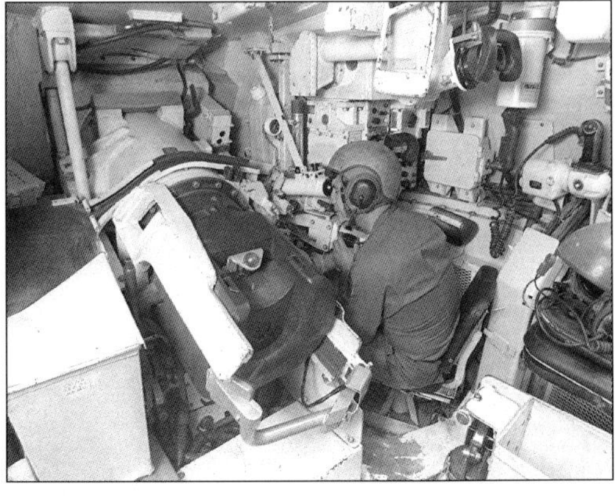

(above) A view inside the XM1's turret as the gunner checks the 105mm gun. (NARA: Eddie McCrossan)

(above) One of the Low-Rate Initial Production (LRIP) XM1s goes through its paces at the US Armor School, Fort Knox, KY, in December 1979. (NARA: Eddie McCrossan)

(below) Another view of the XM1, identifiable by its more complex mounting for the commander's M2HB .50cal, taken at the same time. (NARA: Eddie McCrossan)

(bottom) The first XM1 to be accepted into service now stands at the US Army Ordnance Museum, Aberdeen, MA. (US Army Ordnance Museum)

An M1 of 2-5 Cavalry at the U.S. Armor School, Fort Knox, KY, in January 1983. This tank is camouflaged in a U.S. and Europe, Summer MERDC (Mobility Equipment Research & Design Command) scheme. (NARA: Steve Catlin)

M1 AND IPM1

The first XM1 was built by the Lima Tank Plant and presented to the US Army in February 1980. Attending the ceremony were the family of the late General Creighton Abrams, a decorated veteran tank commander of World War II and the Korean War and one of the US Army commanders during the Vietnam War. Abrams had been appointed Chief of Staff of the US Army in 1972 and he was instrumental in the early stages of the new tank's development. In 1974, however, he had died of lung cancer. The first XM1 was christened 'Thunderbolt', the same name given to the M4s Abrams had ridden as commander of the 37th Tank Battalion during World War II. The US Army's new main battle tank would henceforth by known as the Abrams. Full production of the M1 was finally authorised in February the following year, with the Block I production of 30 tanks per month each at both the Lima and Detroit tank factories. With multiple shifts it was possible to produce a combined total of 150 tanks a month at both plants. On 31 March 1982 the first M1s were accepted into service by the US Army. Production of the M1 continued at both plants and by the summer of 1982, 585 tanks had been produced and delivered, equipping three tank battalions in Germany and two in the United States.

The M1 was armed with the 105mm M68A1 rifled tank gun, a licence-built version of the British Royal Ordnance L7 gun. The gun was fully stabilised and capable of engaging and destroying targets at a range of one mile during daytime or night. The turret bustle and hull could store 55 rounds of 105mm

A good view of the turret rear on an M1 serving with 1-11 ACR in Germany during 1985. A system of canvas straps was fitted to the rear of M1 to hold the crew's personal gear until the fitting of the external stowage rack as part of the Product Improvement Program. (NARA: TSgt. Boyd Belchin)

M1s move up to take their place in a live-fire exercise at Fort Knox in December 1989 to test the new M298A1 'Silver Bullet' APFSDS round. (NARA: J.D. Holmes Jr)

ammunition. Its secondary armament consisted of the commander's M2HB .50cal, a pintle-mounted and a coaxial 7.62mm M240 machine gun. It was powered by the Honeywell AGT1500C multi-fuel turbine engine, a distinct new departure in US tank design. The new tank weighed 54 tons and was protected by Burlington composite armour.

The initial LRIP Abrams were delivered to 2-5 Cavalry, 1st Cavalry Division, based at Fort Hood, Texas. The new tank was a controversial introduction to the inventory of the US Army. To many in the media it was a symbol of the Reagan administration's militarism and an expensive and unnecessary indulgence, but the military's initial reaction was largely positive. A change quickly introduced at Fort Hood was a redesign of the last side skirt panel. Field trials had shown that side skirt covering the drive sprocket quickly led to a build-up of mud. A new cut-back version was introduced, although the original configuration continued to be seen throughout the M1's early service history and it is quite common, even today, to see the Abrams with the final side skirt panel removed.

In 1982 Chrysler, the original designer and manufacturer of the M1 was forced to sell its military product division and the US government approved its sale to General Dynamics Corporation, the principal military contractor for the government. General Dynamics Land Systems (GDLS) would go onto develop the M1 throughout its history with the US Army and later Marine Corps. In all, between 1980 and January 1985, Chrysler and then GDLS built 2,734 M1 Abrams at their Detroit and Lima plants.

Even before the first M1s had left the Lima plant, the US Army was well aware of the shortcomings of the 105mm gun against the latest generation of Soviet armour, especially the T-64 and T-72. As we have seen, in the initial stages of development some consideration had been given to equipping the M1 from the beginning with the 120mm Rheinmetall gun. Improvements in 105mm ammunition, notably the introduction in 1979 of a depleted uranium core Armour Piercing Fin Stabilised Discarding Sabot (APFSDS) round, had ensured that the initial production run of the M1 retained adequate firepower to deal with any potential Warsaw Pact enemy. Nevertheless, American developers continued to work on their own 120mm tank gun. In 1981 the US obtained a licence to manufacture its own simplified version of the Rheinmetall gun, the M256 and in March the first 120mm-armed prototypes, named the M1E1, were delivered. The M1E1 had a number of other developments that were gathered together under the Abrams Product Improvement Program. Most notably this included increased armour on the front, which lengthened the turret by some nine inches. This additional weight also resulted in improvements to the suspension, transmission and final drives. The final improvement, and the most notable in terms of external differences, to the Block I tank was the addition of a rear external stowage rack on the rear turret bustle. This was in direct response to complaints from front-line tankers about the lack of stowage, at least compared to the M60.

In October 1984 the changes planned for the M1E1, with the exception of the new 120mm main gun, associated ammunition stowage arrangements, and a new Nuclear, Biological, Chemical (NBC) crew protection system, were introduced to the M1s being manufactured at Lima and Detroit. This variant of the Abrams was known as the Improved Performance M1 (IPM1). From October until May 1986 a total of 894 IPM1s were produced and they continued to equip the tank battalions of the US Army in both Germany and the United States as they transitioned from M60A3s.

A USMC M1A1 photographed at Camp Lejeune, NC, in January 1993. Only one regular and one reserve battalion of the USMC's tank force were equipped with M1A1s during Operation Desert Storm and the remainder of the force swapped their aging M60A1 RISE Passives for the Abrams on their return to the United States. (NARA)

M1A1

The final decision to up-gun the Abrams with the 120mm gun was taken in December 1984 and in August the following year the first deliveries of the newly named M1A1 were made to units in Germany. The basic differences between the M1A1 and its M1 and IPM1 predecessors were the main gun and the NBC system. Early in the development of the M1E1 consideration had been given to fitting a Commander's Independent Thermal Viewer (CITV), which would allow the tank commander to view the images from the gunner's thermal sight. Cost was the major factor in not adopting this on the production M1A1s, but a circular cut-out on the hull roof was put in place to facilitate later adoption. The M1E1's designers also considered an auxiliary power unit (APU), fitted at the rear of the turret, which would allow the fire control and other electronic systems to run while the engine was turned off without draining the tank's batteries. Again cost prevented this being incorporated into the initial production run but some tanks had been fitted with APUs by the time of Operation Desert Storm.

Since 1985 several variants of the M1A1 have served, and continue to serve, with the US Army and USMC. In all, 4,771 M1A1s were built between December 1984 and April 1993. The variants of the M1A1 in service with the US Army and USMC are as follows:

M1A1: baseline production of the M1A1, armed with the M256 120mm gun with stowage for forty rounds of ammunition. 2,338 M1A1s were manufactured by GDLS.

M1A1 HA: from May 1988 new M1A1s were manufactured with a depleted uranium (DU) insert between the two large armour compartments of the turret front. This was in addition to the ceramic layers of the original Burlington composite armour and added about an extra ton to the overall weight of the tank. 1,234 M1A1 HA tanks were manufactured from May 1988 until May 1991.

M1A1 Common: in 1990 the USMC decided to adopt the M1A1 as its standard MBT. In November 1990 a series of upgrades were added to the M1A1 HA, three of which – the Deep Water Fording Kit (DWFK), additional tie-down points, and a position locating reference system – were USMC requirements. USMC M1A1s were also fitted with the distinctive M257 turret smoke discharger, which differed from the US Army's in having eight launchers as opposed to the Army's six. The original USMC procurement was for 215 tanks, later expanded to 445 with transfers from the US Army.

M1A1 HA+: from May 1991 M1A1s were manufactured with an additional DU insert on top of that fitted to the original M1A1 HA. 834 tanks thus configured were manufactured up to April 1993.

Already from 1989 the performance of the M1A1 was being enhanced by new ammunition, the M298A1 APFSDS 'Silver Bullet' round. As the 1990s progressed, various other upgrades came online, mainly electronic. In the early 1990s 1,500 M1A1s were fitted with APUs. One of the most important of the electronic enhancements was the Force XXI Battle Command Brigade and Below programme. In 2001-2 funding was secured for 1,535 M1A1s to be thus upgraded. Central to this was the Blue Force Tracker, enabling commanders to know their tank's position on the battlefield relative to all other friendly forces. Another obvious external change was the introduction of Combat Identification Panels, which provided a distinctive signature when viewed through thermal sights, allowing friendly forces to be quickly identified on a fluid battlefield. By the late 1990s, however, the Army's fleet of M1A1 was ready for a more extensive overhaul of its mechanical and automotive components. The Abrams Integrated Management Program for the 21st Century (AIM XXI) was designed to bring those M1A1s not being rebuilt as M1A2s to parity

An M1A1 AIM of 1-77 Armor rolls through a wintery-looking Grafenwoehr Training Area in February 2007. (US Army: SPC Joe Alger)

with the latest generation of Abrams main battle tanks.

M1A1 AIM: this was a rolling series of modifications carried out from July 2000 to the US Army's fleet of M1A1s. The most important modifications were addition of the Blue Force Tracker and other digital upgrades, as well as a thermal sight for the .50cal M2HB machine gun and an infantry phone at the rear of the tank.

M1A1 SA: the M1A1 Situational Awareness (SA) tank. As well as the electronic upgrades included in AIM XXI, the M1A1 SA benefited from the Total Integrated Engine Revitalization (TIGER) Program, which totally rebuilt the tank's engine to a 'as-new' standard in preference to the costly acquisition of the cancelled new LV-100-5 gas turbine engine for the Abrams fleet. The M1A1 SA also includes a new Forward Looking Infrared Sight (FLIR) for the gunner, improved laser rangefinder and a Stabilised Commander's Weapon Station (SCWS) with thermal sight. The first M1A1 SA tanks were delivered in March 2009 and by the end of the year 958 M1A1 SA served with National Guard units, the 1st and 2nd Infantry Divisions and as pre-positioned equipment in Kuwait and Korea.

M1A1 FEP: the USMC did not adopt the same modifications and upgrade programs at the same time to their Abrams fleet as the US Army. Between 2004 and 2007 they continued to receive additional M1A1s as their fleet took casualties and experienced combat fatigue as a result of the Iraq War. From 2005 until 2010 the USMC reconfigured 386 tanks as part of the Firepower Enhancement Program (FEP). This included new thermal sights, a far-target location system and a thermal sight with a new and distinctive USMC SCWS. This was followed in recent years by a series of SA enhancements and, most recently, by an Improved Side Armor (ISA kit).

With these improvements the M1A1 FEP is expected to serve as the armoured backbone of the USMC for the foreseeable future. Equally, the M1A1 SA will continue to equip the National Guard Armored Brigade Combat Teams of the US Army into the next decade and beyond.

An M1A1 SA of Charlie Company, 1-118th Combined Arms Battalion, South Carolina Army National Guard, conducts gunnery exercises on the ranges at Fort Stewart, GA, in April 2014. Note the SCWS with thermal sight and loader's armour protection. (US Army: Sgt. Brian Calhoun)

M1A2 SEP V2s of 1-66 Armor at the Hohenfels Training Area, Germany, during Exercise Combined Resolve VIII in June 2017. (US Army: Spc. Gage Hull)

In October 1989 approval was given for the next stage of the Abrams' development: M1A1E1 or M1A2. The salient features of the new variant were the Commander's Independent Thermal Viewer (CITV) fitted as standard and a new Improved Commander's Weapon Station (ICWS). Other changes were largely electronic, including a GPS positioning system and an electronically integrated information system. The commissioning of the M1A2, of course, coincided with the end of the Cold War and serious doubts over the need for any further MBT production in the United States. In 1990 the United States agreed to sell the M1A2 to Saudi Arabia, but the Detroit Tank Plant closed the following year, leaving Lima (in 2017 renamed the Joint Systems Manufacturing Center) as the only US tank factory to build new Abrams and recondition and convert the existing tank fleet. The US Army's acquisition of the M1A2 began in April 1990 with the last 62 M1A1s on the production line finished as A2. The initial order was for 2,296 new M1A2s but only 77 new tanks had been built up to 1995, while 998 older M1 and IPM1s had been rebuilt to M1A2 standard. The M1A2 was fielded by the US Army in three distinct variants:

M1A2: the demand for an auxiliary power unit (APU), enabling the Abrams to run its electronic systems even when the engine was turned off, had been discussed in the 1980s, but by the early 1990s the need for an APU was clear. Such units were added to M1A1s between 1991 and 1994, but the US Army decided to wait for a more integrated solution. Nevertheless, in 1997 336 M1A2s had an external APU fitted to left side of the turret bustle rack.

M1A2 SEP: the System Enhancement Program (SEP) was a major programme to enhance the US Army's M1A2 fleet beginning in 1999. As well as 240 newly built tanks, the SEP was applied to all existing M1A1 and M1A2 Abrams as they

An M1A2 SEP V2 of 3-66 Armor at the National Training Centre, Fort Irwin, CA, in February 2018. The tank features the CROWS-LP (Common Remotely Operated Weapon Station – Low Profile), a controversial addition to the Abrams fleet which was ordered to be removed in March 2016, although as these photos show it remains in service. (US Army: Esmerelda Cervantes)

An M1A2 SEP V2 of 1-16 Infantry, 1st Armored Brigade Combat Team, 1st Infantry Division, arrives in Romania in February 2019 for the start of NATO exercises. Note the turret mountings for the M32 ERA tiles. (US Army: Spc Yon Trimble)

entered the Lima plant for refurbishment. The most important changes to the M1A2 SEP were internal, concerned to bring the Abrams up to speed with the latest in digital communications and fire control systems. It included a new command and control system, new laser range finding equipment and thermal imaging capabilities, as well as new depleted uranium armour inserts. Externally the most important change from the M1A2 was the Under Armor APU, negating the need for the APU carried in the turret bustle stowage rack. The first M1A2 SEPs equipped the 4th Infantry Division in May 2000 and for Operation Iraqi Freedom the US Army fielded a mixed fleet of M1A1 HA, M1A2 and M1A2 SEP.

M1A2 SEP V2: the decision to cancel the Future Combat System program in 2009 guaranteed that the Abrams would remain the principal warfighting machine of the US Army for decades to come. That year the first unit, 4th Brigade, 1st Cavalry Division, was equipped with latest variant of the Abrams to see service. The principal external difference on the SEP V2 is the Common Remote Operated Weapons System (CROWS). Other changes are mainly internal and relate to the tank's digital systems.

Future Developments: with the Abrams set to serve in the US Army for many years to come, the M1A2 is currently going through a series of evolutionary changes. Improvements included the better power management systems and the CREW/Duke 3 IED jammer (discernible by its prominent aerials). These and other Engineering Change Proposals (ECP) constitute the SEP V3 which is currently under trials with the US Army. In September the Army is expected to begin trials of the SEP V4, which will incorporate more systems improvements, as well as improved frontal armour and new ammunition for the 120mm gun. Tests are also underway of the Israeli-manufactured Trophy Active Protection System, designed to intercept and destroy incoming Anti-Tank Guided Missiles (ATGM). In this way the Abrams, designed to meet the challenges of the Cold War, will remain the most effective main battle tank on the battlefields of the 21st-century.

In February 2019 the US Army revealed photos of the M1A2 SEP V3 with the additional frontal turret armour, M19 side ERA and the Trophy Active Protection System installed. (US Army)

THE COLD WAR

In the early 1980s the US Army in Europe's (USAREUR) organisation and tactics to meet the anticipated Warsaw Pact adversary were undergoing fundamental change. The US planners believed that current NATO organisation and plans did not meet the challenge of the rapid armoured advance that was at the heart of Warsaw Pact doctrine. Soviet tanks, it was feared, would be at the heart of western Europe's industrial and population centres within hours of the start of an attack, rendering impossible NATO's planned tactical nuclear response. The US Army's new doctrine, known as AirLand Battle, therefore envisaged an aggressive, combined arms response to any Warsaw Pact invasion of NATO territory. A host of new, technologically sophisticated weapons systems, employed within a new command structure – the Division 86 structure – would take the fight to the enemy, with deep strikes against their rear echelon, in order to buy time to bring reinforcements from the continental United States and elsewhere in NATO.

At the centre of this new organisational structure and tactics was the M1 Abrams main battle tank. Alongside the Bradley Fighting Vehicle, Apache Attack Helicopters, the Multiple-Launch Rocket System, and a host of new munitions (such as the Copperhead cannon-launched guided munition and the Cruise Missile), the Abrams provided the backbone of the new Division 86 structure. Under the Division 86 structure each tank battalion comprised an HQ, a Headquarters company and four tank companies. The HQ company would have six M3 Bradley Cavalry Fighting Vehicles, a mortar and support platoons, with two M1s attached as battalion command. Each of the four tank companies comprised three platoons of four M1s, with two attached to the company HQ. This represented a considerable change in US armoured force organisation, replacing the previous structure of three companies per battalion, with platoons of five tanks. The Division 86 structure provided for 58 MBTs to each US Army tank battalion. The M1 was the first of these weapons systems to enter service with the US Army and the initial deliveries of the new Main Battle Tank were made to 2- and 3-64 Armor, 1st Brigade, 3rd Infantry Division in early 1982.

By September 1982 the M1s of 1st Brigade were set to make their debut during

The 'Soviet Big 7': a US information poster distributed to units in Germany in 1981. As the new decade dawned, NATO was very much on the defensive, searching for new weapons and tactics that would halt the much-vaunted armoured might of the Warsaw Pact. (NARA)

An atmospheric image of M1s of 2-64 Armor executing the type of rapid manoeuvre that made such an impact on both the Americans and their NATO allies during Exercise Carbine Fortress in 1982. (NARA: Spc Buck Brignano)

Exercise Carbine Fortress, part of the annual REFORGER (Return of Forces to Germany) exercise. The tanks of 2- and 3-64 Armor were first employed as the defending Blue Force against an attack of the Orange Force's 4th Canadian Mechanized Brigade Group. The Abrams quickly proved its abilities with a swift and decisive thrust into the rear areas of the Canadian Battlegroup. As one of the Canadian officers observed: 'One minute it was quiet and no enemy was in sight, but the next minute you're overrun and choked by a silent, swift opponent'. The speed and relative quiet of the Abrams' turbine engine earned it the nickname 'whispering death' among envious NATO tankers. Significantly, however, observers at the time commented on the apparent lack of appreciation of the effect of enemy airpower by American troops and NATO commanders in general. It was also noted that the units did not have sufficient tools or spare parts to cope with the inevitable breakdowns of the new tanks. Nevertheless, as the commander of 3rd Infantry Division noted at the conclusion of Exercise Carbine Fortress, 'Operationally the M1 Abrams exceeded our expectations during REFORGER 82. The fighting power of the new weapon system turned out to be so big that new perspectives will be necessary in the deployment of armoured units'.

The following year the crews of 3-64 Armor got to test their Abrams against

An M1 of 3-64 Armor advances to contact during Exercise Carbine Fortress 82. (NARA: SSgt Bob Simons)

the best NATO armour and crews in the biennial Canadian Army Trophy, bringing together men and machines from across both CENTAG (Central Army Group) and NORTHAG (Northern Army Group). The M1s came second behind the Bundeswehr's Leopard 1A1s, although interestingly a crew from 2-66 Armor equipped with the M60A1, disparagingly dubbed 'the Dinosaurs' before the competition, came in third. This highlighted that while new technology was important, the individual gunnery and other skills of the tank crew remained paramount in even the most modern MBTs. It was an important lesson for US commanders that even within the new Division 86 structure victory still depended on the man behind the gun.

In August 1983 a second unit, 11th Armored Cavalry Regiment, traded in some of its M60A3s for the new M1. It begun Exercise Confident Enterprise, part of REFORGER 83, with a mixed complement of M1s in its 1st Squadron and M60A3s in its 2nd and 3rd. For the first time the new doctrine of the AirLand Battle was employed fully. 11 ACR successfully blunted the Orange Forces' first attack echelon, but a large number of 1st Squadron's M1s were subsequently cut off and 'destroyed' by the M60A1s of 3 ACR. The following year saw more tank units equipped with the M1, and in February 1984 the first M3 Bradley Cavalry Fighting Vehicles were deployed as reconnaissance vehicles for the armoured battalions as part of the new Division 86 structure. Later that year, 1- and 3-67 Armor, 1st Brigade, 2nd US Armored Division employed the M1, M2 Bradley Infantry Fighting Vehicle and the M3 Bradley CFV together for the first time against British forces in Exercise Lionheart 84.

In 1985 the new IPM1 began to be delivered to the tank units of USAREUR. For REFORGER 85 1- and 3-33 Armor, 2nd Brigade 3rd US Armored Division were fully equipped with the Abrams and other AFVs in accordance with the Division 86 structure, while the 1st and 3rd Brigades were still equipped with M60A3s. Steadily more and more units replaced their M60s with the M1, but this process was not yet complete when the M1/IPM1 was replaced in frontline units by the 120mm-armed M1A1 in 1989. In 1987 the Abrams once again proved its abilities during the annual Canadian Army Trophy. Two years earlier 3-64 Armor had competed for the first time in their new IPM1 tanks, but poor weather was partly responsible for them coming in second place behind the new German Leopard 2. However, in the next competition and for the first time in 24 years the laurels were taken by an American tank platoon from 4-8 Cavalry operating IPM1s, while the Abrams of 3-64 Armor came third behind the Leopard 2A4s of the Bundeswehr's Panzerbattalion 124. Significantly, the Americans decided not to put together a team of 'super tankers' with previous CAT experience, but to select a team that was representative of the general capabilities of the Abrams-equipped US tank battalions. That said, and despite American claims that this was a competition and not a test of each nation's tank forces, the Abrams' platoons underwent a month-long schedule of intensive field and classroom-based training to ensure their success. In the same year, Bradley crews from 1-11 ACR also won the prestigious Boeseleger Challenge Cup, organised by the Bundeswehr to test the capabilities of NATO reconnaissance platoons.

In June 1987 US President Ronald Reagan famously challenged Mikhail Gorbachev, the Soviet leader, to 'tear down' the Berlin Wall at a speech delivered from the Brandenburg Gate. The previous two years had seen a

text continued on page 45

A rear view of a 3-64 Armor M1 paused and awaiting orders during Exercise Carbine Fortress 82. (NARA: SSgt Bob Simons)

1. M1, 'Company Delta', 1st Squadron, 11th Armored Cavalry Regiment, Exercise Confident Enterprise, Germany, September 1983. The M1s of 11 ACR were finished, in common with all early service Abrams, in Forest Green FS 34079. The tank was then covered in locally applied mud in a rather elaborate geometric pattern.

2. M1, 'Company Mauler', 1st Squadron, 11th Armored Cavalry Regiment, Exercise Central Guardian, Germany, January 1985. The winter in Germany in January 1985 was one of the coldest on record. Both men and machines suffered in the intense cold, snow and ice. The Abrams of 1-11 ACR acted as Blue Force. The tanks were camouflaged which a water-based chalk whitewash in a random fashion which quickly washed. An after-exercise report in *Armor* magazine concluded that whitewashing tanks was of little utility in the conditions of the German winter.

COLOUR PROFILES BY SLAWOMIR ZAJACZKOWSKI

3

3. M1A1, 4th Battalion, 66th Armor Regiment, 3rd Phantom Brigade, 1st Armored Division, Operation Desert Storm, Kuwait, February 1991. The tanks of 4-66 Armor were instrumental in the defeat of the Iraqi Republican Guard at the battle of Medina Ridge on 27 February 1991. The M1A1s of the US Army during Operation Desert Storm were all finished in Desert Tan FS33446. Each unit used a distinctive system of chevrons (the ubiquitous tactical symbol of the coalition forces) and numbers to identify different companies. *(Photo: NARA: SSgt. Robert L. Reeve)*

4. M1A1, 'Charlie Company', 2nd Battalion, 68th Armor Regiment, 'Task Force Eagle', 1st Armored Division, Bosnia-Herzegovina, August 1996. The M1A1s of Task Force Eagle were all painted in the standard three-tone NATO camouflaged, which had been introduced to USAREUR IN 1987. It was known as 'Europe-1' in the US Army and consisted of Green 383 (FS 34094), Brown 383 (FS 30051) and Black (FS 37030). It was factory applied with a spray gun and slightly feathered. The tank also has an IFOR marking stencilled on, as well as a tactical marking, '63', which probably identifies the company. *(Photo NARA: SSgt. Nicholas Blair)*

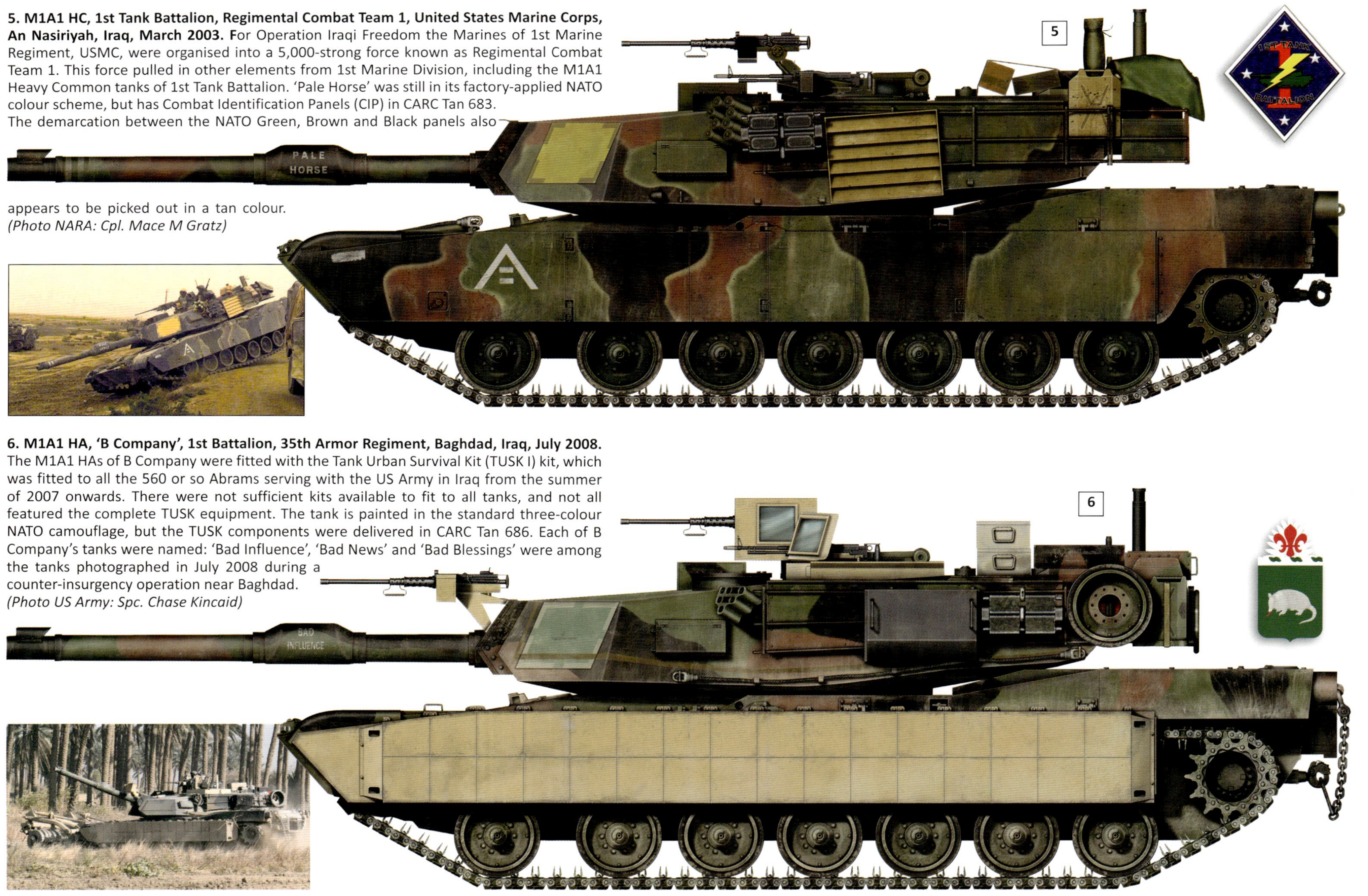

5. M1A1 HC, 1st Tank Battalion, Regimental Combat Team 1, United States Marine Corps, An Nasiriyah, Iraq, March 2003. For Operation Iraqi Freedom the Marines of 1st Marine Regiment, USMC, were organised into a 5,000-strong force known as Regimental Combat Team 1. This force pulled in other elements from 1st Marine Division, including the M1A1 Heavy Common tanks of 1st Tank Battalion. 'Pale Horse' was still in its factory-applied NATO colour scheme, but has Combat Identification Panels (CIP) in CARC Tan 683. The demarcation between the NATO Green, Brown and Black panels also appears to be picked out in a tan colour. *(Photo NARA: Cpl. Mace M Gratz)*

6. M1A1 HA, 'B Company', 1st Battalion, 35th Armor Regiment, Baghdad, Iraq, July 2008. The M1A1 HAs of B Company were fitted with the Tank Urban Survival Kit (TUSK I) kit, which was fitted to all the 560 or so Abrams serving with the US Army in Iraq from the summer of 2007 onwards. There were not sufficient kits available to fit to all tanks, and not all featured the complete TUSK equipment. The tank is painted in the standard three-colour NATO camouflage, but the TUSK components were delivered in CARC Tan 686. Each of B Company's tanks were named: 'Bad Influence', 'Bad News' and 'Bad Blessings' were among the tanks photographed in July 2008 during a counter-insurgency operation near Baghdad. *(Photo US Army: Spc. Chase Kincaid)*

7. M1A2 SEP V2, 1st Battalion, 66th Armor Regiment, 3rd Armored Brigade Combat Team, 4th Infantry Division, Grafenwoehr Training Area, Germany, March 2017. The Abrams of 1-66 Armor were fitted with the Abrams Reactive Armor Tiles (ARAT) I and ARAT II, respectively the M19 Explosive Reactive Armor (ERA) tiles and the M32 Explosive Reactive Armor (ERA) tiles. Each armour skirt contains 31 M19 ERA tiles and on top of these are installed 32 M32 tiles that make up the ARAT II kit. On the turret there are ten tiles on the left-hand side of the turret and eleven on the right-hand side. There is also an additional upper row of turret tiles that includes six more M32 per turret side. *(Photo: US Army: Andreas Kreuzer)*

8. M1A2 SEP V2, 2nd Squadron, 5th Cavalry Regiment, 1st Armored Brigade Combat Team, 1st Cavalry Division, Zagan, Poland, February 2018. The M1A2s of 2-5 Cavalry retained their CARC Tan 686 factory finish when on rotation as part of NATO's Battlegroup Poland. Note the tactical marking, vehicle names stencilled onto the barrel and the unit insignia on the fume extractor. *(Photo: US Army: Eugen Warkentin)*

9. M1A2 SEP V2, 1st Battalion, 63rd Armor Regiment, 2nd Armored Brigade Combat Team, 1st Infantry Division, Exercise Combined Resolve X, Grafenwoehr Training Area, Germany, April 2018. The Abrams of 1-63 Armor, like many of the other AFVs of 2nd Armored Brigade Combat Team, were painted in Bronze Green RAL6031 over their factory-standard CARC Tan 686. Judging from the way the painted chipped and wore away, this wasn't the more durable CARC Green 683 applied to some US military vehicles. The tanks also wore a prominent set of geometric tactical symbols that denoted company and platoons. These were applied by masking the CARC Tan when the Bronze Green was applied. *(Photo US Army: Spc. Dustin D. Biven)*

10. M1A2 SEP V2, 2nd Battalion, 70th Armor Regiment, 2nd Armored Brigade Combat Team, 1st Infantry Division, 'Strong Europe Tank Challenge', Grafenwoehr Training Area, Germany, June 2018. The annual Strong Europe Tank Challenge saw a platoon of Abrams from 2-70 Armor take on tank crews from a range of NATO and partner nations. The tanks had a solid coat of CARC Green 683 and a prominent white star, the first time US tanks had worn this marking in Europe since the 1950s. The prominent marking on the turret front references the 'Big Red One', the 1st Infantry Division. *(Photo US Army: Staff Sgt. Wallace Bonner)*

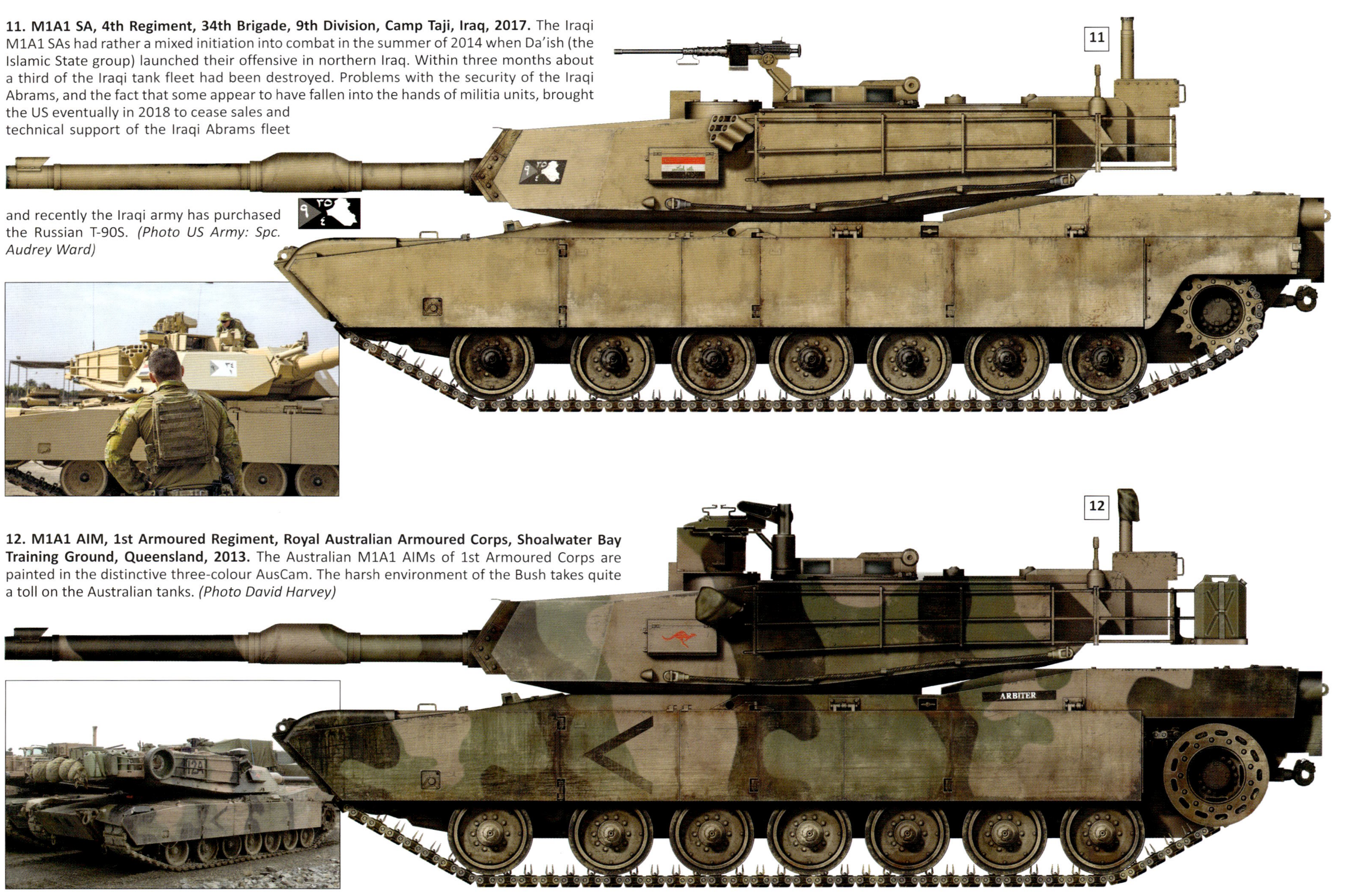

11. M1A1 SA, 4th Regiment, 34th Brigade, 9th Division, Camp Taji, Iraq, 2017. The Iraqi M1A1 SAs had rather a mixed initiation into combat in the summer of 2014 when Da'ish (the Islamic State group) launched their offensive in northern Iraq. Within three months about a third of the Iraqi tank fleet had been destroyed. Problems with the security of the Iraqi Abrams, and the fact that some appear to have fallen into the hands of militia units, brought the US eventually in 2018 to cease sales and technical support of the Iraqi Abrams fleet and recently the Iraqi army has purchased the Russian T-90S. *(Photo US Army: Spc. Audrey Ward)*

12. M1A1 AIM, 1st Armoured Regiment, Royal Australian Armoured Corps, Shoalwater Bay Training Ground, Queensland, 2013. The Australian M1A1 AIMs of 1st Armoured Corps are painted in the distinctive three-colour AusCam. The harsh environment of the Bush takes quite a toll on the Australian tanks. *(Photo David Harvey)*

The model was based on the old Tamiya M1 turret and Dragon's M1 Panther II hull with a set of Trumpeter individual-link tracks.

M1

2ND BATTALION, 64TH ARMOR REGIMENT, EXERCISE CARBINE FORTRESS, GERMANY, SEPTEMBER 1982

1/35 SCALE TAMIYA/ DRAGON

JOHN MURPHY

An M1 of 2-64 Armor storms across the German plain during Exercise Carbine Fortress 82. (NARA: Spc. Buck Brignano)

M1A2

1ST SQUADRON, 3RD ARMORED CAVALRY REGIMENT, 'TASK FORCE RIFLES', IRAQ 2003

1/48 SCALE
TAMIYA
JOAQUIN GARCIA GAZQUEZ

An M1A2 fitted with a mine plow of 2nd Squadron, 3 ACR, tows another M1A2 disabled by an IED during Operation Iraqi Freedom. (Jacob Troy)

Tamiya's Quarterscale M1A2 is typical of kits from the Japanese manufacturer: accurate dimensions and sharp moulding make the kit a pleasure to build out of the box.

USMC M1A1 HEAVY COMMON

BRAVO COMPANY, 1ST TANK BATTALION, UNITED STATES MARINE CORPS, IRAQ 2003

1/35 SCALE

CHRIS JERRETT

A USMC M1A1 of 1st Tank Battalion turns a corner along Highway 9 near Ad Diwaniya during Operation Iraqi Freedom in April 2003. (USMC photo by Sgt Paul L. Anstine)

The model is built from the excellent Dragon M1A1 kit (ref. 3585), with some additions from Tamiya's M1A2 with the Perfect Scale Modellbau USMC resin update-set for the Dragon kit (ref. 35080) and some scratchbuilt additions.

The model was painted with Tamiya acrylic paint. A Red-Brown undercoat provided an effective pre-shade, then Dark Yellow was sprayed from above leaving small traces of the Red Brown showing through. Deck Tan provided the highlights, while the lost yellow hue was restored with a coat of Tamiya's Clear Yellow.

Most of the weathering, including the paint chips and streaks, was achieved with various applications of oil paints.

1:35 MODERN AFV SERIES
M1A1 AIM
DRAGON
B3-1

M1A1HA

CHARLIE COMPANY, 1ST BATTALION, 37TH ARMOR REGIMENT, 1ST ARMORED DIVISION, IRAQ 2003

1/35 SCALE DRAGON

MARK CHISHOLM

An M1A1 of 1-37 Armor Regiment at the Friedberg Training Area in Germany, September 2002. Less than a year later these tanks were instrumental in the capture of Baghdad by US forces during Operation Iraqi Freedom. (NARA: Eric Steen)

M1A2 SEP TUSK II

COMPANY C, 1ST BATTALION, 68TH ARMOR REGIMENT 4TH INFANTRY DIVISION, BAGHDAD 2008

1/35 SCALE
RYEFIELD MODEL
VORYA HEIDARYAN

Soldiers of 1-66 Armor, 4th Infantry Division, fit Abrams Reactive Armor Tiles (ARAT), part of the TUSK II suite, to an M1A2 SEP V2 at the Grafenwoehr training area in 2017. (US Army: Visual Information Specialist Gerhard Seuffert)

M1A2 SEP

A COMPANY, 3RD BATTALION, 64TH ARMOR REGIMENT, 4TH INFANTRY DIVISION, IRAQ 2003

1/72 SCALE FLYHAWK

ARTUR WALACHOWSKI

An M1A2 SEP of 3-64 Armor Regiment, 4th Infantry Division, stands watch during Operation Iraqi Freedom. (NARA photo)

In 1/72 scale there is a range of accessories, essential to accurately model any modern US armour subject, available from a variety of manufacturers like CMK and T Model.

M1A2 SEP V2

2ND BATTALION, 70TH ARMOR REGIMENT, 2ND ARMORED BRIGADE COMBAT TEAM, 1ST INFANTRY DIVISION, GERMANY 2018

1/35 SCALE ACADEMY

DAVID GRUMMITT

Soldiers of the 2-227th Aviation Regiment, 1st Air Cavalry Brigade, 1st Cavalry Division, and 1-18 Infantry Regiment, 2nd Armored Brigade Combat Team, 1st Infantry Division, work together to refuel an M1A2 during a simulated jump forward area refueling point (FARP) exercise at Hohenfels Training Area, Germany, in January 2018. (US Army: Sgt. Gregory T. Summers)

(above) Tamiya 35158 (right) Dragon 3533

The M1 Abrams is one of the most popular subjects for plastic kit manufacturers and producers of aftermarket accessories, with all the main production variants available in all the popular scales from a wide variety of manufacturers. In modelling terms, the basic M1 Abrams is a reasonably straightforward subject, yet there is wide variance in the available kits in terms of detail, accuracy and ease of construction.

In this section I have listed the various full kits of the M1 Abrams available, with some comments based on my own experience of building some of them and through speaking with other modellers. I've also listed some – but by no means all – of the accessories and aftermarket details that can be used to enhance the appearance of any Abrams model.

(above) Italeri 6438
(below) Tamiya 35269
(right) Academy 13202

FULL KITS

The first 1/35-scale kits of the Abrams were produced in the 1980s with Tamiya releasing their M1 kit (ref. 35124) in 1982. Dimensionally this was pretty sound, but it was designed for motorisation and suffered from some soft and missing details. Academy released a motorised M1 (ref. TA049) in 1986, and ESCI/ERTL released both the M1 (ref. 5020) and M1A1 (ref. 5021) a couple of years later. The first Gulf War prompted a rash of new Abrams releases. Tamiya released an M1A1 with a mine plow (ref. 35158) and without (ref. 35156), while Dragon Models Limited released their first Abrams kit, an M1A1 with Mine Plow (ref. 3516) in 1992. The Dragon kit was also reboxed by Revell (ref. 03004). These kits were an improvement on those of the 80s, but all lacked the characteristic anti-slip texture on the hull and turret. A year later Dragon also released their first M1A2 kit (ref. 3524).

Operation Iraqi Freedom and the second Gulf War prompted another round of reboxing and retooling of 1/35-scale Abrams kits. Dragon reboxed their 1992 kit as M1A1HA (ref. 3533) in 2003, while Italeri offered a newly tooled M1A2 (ref. 6390) in the same year and an M1A1 (ref. 6438) a year later. The M1A2 version of this kit was also reboxed by Airfix (ref. 07361). Tamiya also released an M1A2 (ref. 35269) with some appropriate OIF stowage and marking. Similarly, the old Academy kit was upgraded and released as M1A1 Iraq 2003 (ref. 13202). In 2002 Chinese firm Trumpeter entered the fray, releasing the M1A1HA (ref. 0034), closely followed by the same kit with mine plow (ref. 00335) and mine roller (ref. 0036) and an M1A2 (ref. 0037). Trumpeter's Abrams are often overlooked, but are on a par with the Academy, Italeri and Tamiya kits of the same vintage and include some nice details (such as the blank-firing adapter for the .50cal M2 Browning). All of these kits,

(above) Trumpeter 05135
(right) Dragon Models Limited 3536
(below) Tamiya 35326

and the Panther II Mine Clearing Tank (ref. 00346), were reboxed in a special '5 in 1' kit released in 2008 (ref. 05135).

In 2005 Dragon released their M1 Panther II Mine Detection and Clearing Vehicle (ref. 3534). This included an accurate, newly tooled M1 hull and it seemed that the venerable Tamiya M1 could soon be retired in favour of a new 105mm gun tank. It was not to be and instead, the following year, Dragon offered a newly tooled M1A1 AIM (ref. 3535). This was followed in 2007 by a new M1A2 (ref. 3536). These are superb kits: detailed, dimensionally accurate and have an unprecedented range of accessories and marking options. On the downside, they are markedly more challenging to build than the Tamiya, Academy or Italeri kits and the busy instructions require careful study. The various in-service upgrades kept the kit manufacturers busy and in 2012 Tamiya upgraded their M1A2 with the TUSK II kit (ref. 35326) and two years later Dragon raised the bar again with their comprehensive M1A2 SEP V2 (ref. 3556).

2016-17 saw three new manufacturers and four newly tooled M1 Abrams kits in 1/35 scale. Academy released a completely newly tooled M1A2 V2 TUSK II (ref. 13298). This is a superb kit with some wonderful details and an ease of build that rivals Tamiya. The following year another version of this was released (ref. 13504) with some new markings and, best of all, the inclusion of DEF. Model's superb T158 individual link tracks. Academy is probably the best all-round Abrams kit available in 1/35, but it is closely challenged by the releases from Meng Model and Ryefield Model. Meng also began by releasing an M1A2 SEP TUSK kit (ref. TS-026). This is a beautifully moulded kit with some complex individual track links, but it falters in comparison with Academy simply because it does not include the clear hub caps for the roadwheels. Meng Model followed this up by a release of the M1A1 AIM (ref. TS-032). Again, this is a superb kit that can be built as either a USMC M1A1 AIM or a US Army M1A1 with TUSK kit. This latter kit is now

(above) Dragon Models Limited 3556
(below) Academy 13504
(right) Meng Model TS-032

Ryefield Model RM5006

(above) Ryefield Model RM5011
(below) Panda Hobby 35038

probably the go-to choice for an M1A1, supplanting the now difficult-to-find Dragon kit. On a par with Meng, however, are the Abrams kits released by Ryefield Model. M1A2 SEP TUSK I/TUSK II/M1A1 TUSK (ref. RM5004) is as comprehensive kit as its name suggests and builds into an excellent and accurate replica of the vehicles seen in the latter stages of the US operation in Iraq. The kit was also reboxed with new link-and-length T156 tracks and other details as M1A1 Desert Storm Edition (ref. RM5006). This is another great kit, but the link-and-length tracks are a little disappointing compared to the finesse of RFM's other offerings. Best of all perhaps, RFM released an M1A1/M1A2 with full interior and engine (ref. RM5007). This really is an excellent kit and offers modellers of the Abrams MBT a unique opportunity to model a maintenance-themed vignette. Alongside the gun tanks, RFM have also released the only plastic kit of the M1 Assault Breacher Vehicle (ref. RM5011). This is one of the most complex and appealing of Abrams-based vehicles and RFM have done a superb job.

A more mixed bag is Panda Hobby's M1 Abrams (ref. 35030) and M1 IP Abrams (ref. 35038). The basic shape of these are sound and they represent a real improvement over the old Tamiya kit. Nevertheless, they suffer from some really soft details, especially around the turret, and some individual-link T156 tracks which have a frustratingly sloppy fit. Indeed, some aspects of the kit are really unusable, but there enough options out there in both plastic and resin to enable modellers wanting to add these early Abrams to their collection to make very presentable models from the Panda kits. Indeed, the Panda Hobby M1 IP is the only game in town for this important part of the Abrams story.

REPLACEMENT TRACKS

There are a number of options if you are looking to replace the kit tracks for a 1/35-scale Abrams, especially important if you're using the older Academy, Italeri or Tamiya kits that have one-piece vinyl tracks. The options for the older T-156 tracks are restricted to those from Armour Track Models (ref. TK-02) and Trumpeter (ref. 02032). These are actually the same set marketed under different brands and are now quite difficult to find. The range of available T-158 replacement tracks is much wider, providing modellers with a range of different levels of complexity and approach. Metal tracks are available from Friulmodel (ref. ATL-155) and Spade Ace (SAT-35132), but the weight and the one-piece manufacture of the white metal tracklink does not really capture the appearance of the real thing. More complex, workable multi-part individual links are available from AFV Club (ref. AF3512), Bronco (ref. AB3522) and Ryefield Models (ref. RM-5009), but probably the most user-friendly option are the individual links from DEF.Model (ref. S35001).

(above) Bronco AB3522
(right) Rye Field Models RM-5009

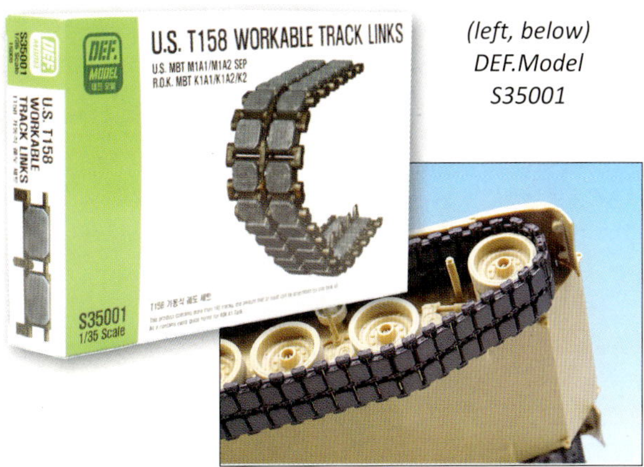

(left, below) DEF.Model S35001

(above) Esci/AMT/ERTL 8070

(above) Hasegawa MA1

SMALL SCALE ABRAMS

The M1 is almost as popular among Small-Scale kit manufacturers as it is among those that specialise in 1/35 scale. In 1986 Esci released an M1 kit in 1/72 scale (ref. 8070). This has been reboxed and new sprues added by several manufacturers over the years, most notably Italeri who used the kit as the basis for their M1 released in 2001 (ref. 7001). The same year Hasegawa released the first of two kits of the Abrams in 1/72 scale, the M1 Abrams (ref. MA1), closely followed by the M1E1 (ref. MA3), the only kit available in any scale of this variant. These were better kits than the Esci ones and were released in three different boxes each, each with different decals. In 1997 Revell released a newly tooled M1A1 (HA) Abrams (ref. 03112). Revell's kit was impressive, confirming their reputation as one of the premier manufacturers of Small-Scale kits. The upper hull and turret had a nicely moulded non-slip texture, while the bustle rack was delicately moulded and the tracks presented as 'link-and-lengths' rather than the vinyl ones included with the Esci and Hasegawa kits. In 2005, in the wake of Operation Iraqi Freedom, Revell released an M1A2 (03146) and in 2011 re-released the M1A1 HA with some new decals.

In 2003 Dragon Models Limited released a newly tooled M1A1 '3rd Infantry Division Iraq 2003' (ref. 7215). While well detailed and comparable in some ways to the older generation of Tamiya and Italeri 1/35-scale kits, the kit was designed to be motorised and a result had some pretty serious scale issues (particularly around the lower hull). The moulding was also a bit hit-and-miss, with the turret bustle rack rails being moulded solid for example. This kit provided the basis for two other Abrams released by Dragon around the same time – an M1A1 with mine plough (ref. 7213) and an M1A2 (ref. 7216) – but which suffered from the same problems. That said, dimensionally speaking, the Dragon Abrams were an improvement on what had come before, surpassed only by the Revell kits. In 2008 Trumpeter joined the fray with their M1A1 Abrams MBT (ref. 07276). These kits are

(above) Revell 03112

(above) Tiger Model 9601

(above) Trumpeter 07278

(below) Flyhawk FH3300

nicely detailed, if a little simplistic (conflating US Army and USMC versions), but were probably second only behind the Revell kits in terms of accuracy. Trumpeter went on to release the M1A1 with mine plough (ref. 07277), mine roller set (ref. 07278), an M1A2 (ref. 07279), and a M1 Panther II Mine Clearing Tank (ref. 07280).

The choice available to Small-Scale modellers wanting to build an M1 Abrams was transformed in 2015 when Tiger Model released their M1A2 SEP TUSK II (ref. 9601). This was of a completely different order to the previous Small-Scale kits with a level of complexity and detail previously only seen in 1/35-scale kits. The kit is nicely moulded, but some of the details look a little chunky and it lacks the anti-slip texture that was so notable a plus for the Revell kit. The tracks were cleverly done, with the inner half of them integrally moulded with the inner half of the road wheels. In some ways the Tiger Model kit was a sign of things to come and Small-Scale Abrams fans finally had their prayers answered in 2017 when Flyhawk Models released their superb M1A2 SEP (ref. FH3300). This, as you can see from Artur Walachowski's model in the gallery pages, took Small-Scale modelling into a new realm, with a level of detail that surpassed that of most the 1/35-scale Abrams kits available. Flyhawk followed this up the following year with a version equipped with a mine clearing blade system (FH3301) and we can only hope for more versions in the future.

(below) The Tiger Model instruction sheet shows the complexity of the new generation of Small-Scale Abrams kits.

(right) The author's Flyhawk M1A2 under construction. As you can see, the level of detail certainly rivals many 1/35-scale kits.

DRAGON ARMOUR

Dragon also released a range of their 1/72 kits fully assembled and painted under the Dragon Armour range. This is their M1A1 Iraq 2003.

OTHER SCALES

1/48 scale ('Quarterscale') is a scale more familiar to aircraft modellers, but in 2001 Academy released a motorised Quarterscale model of the M1A2 (ref. 13002). The same kit was re-released shortly afterwards by Aoshima in both the M1A1 (ref. 00082) and M1A2 (ref. 0080) variants. To be fair, this model was compromised in terms of accuracy and detail by the needs of motorisation, so it was very good news when Tamiya released their M1A2 (ref. 32592) kit in 2017. The kit is dimensionally sound and builds up into a very nice replica, but the choice of a M1A2 variant, rather than the M1A2 SEP which was the prevalent variant that served in OIF and beyond, disappointed a few modellers. Some of the details are also a little soft compared to its 1/35-scale counterpart Fortunately, both Hauler (ref. HLX48385) and Tetra Model Design (ref. 48002) produce photoetched detail sets for the Tamiya kit and the latter, in particular, really lifts the level of detail. British-firm Red Zebra also produce a very set of resin stowage for the Tamiya kit.

At the other end of the scale, both Tamiya and Trumpeter produce 1/16-scale kits of the Abrams. Trumpeter released their kit of the M1A1 AIM (ref. 00926) in 2017 and in the following year followed this up with an M1A2 SEP (ref. 00927). Previously there had been motorised large-scale versions of the Abrams by Heng Long and others, but these and the Tamiya M1A2 (ref. 36212), also released in 2017, were static display models. Both manufacturers' kits have come in for some flak. The biggest problem with the Trumpeter kits is that the kit drive sprockets don't actually fit the T-158 tracks supplied in the kit! The Trumpeter drive sprocket is obviously underscale, but fortunately AFV Modeller have come to the rescue with a resin replacement that fits the Trumpeter tracks perfectly. Unfortunately, the drive sprocket is not the only, nor the most egregious, error on the Trumpeter kits. Both kits are a mixture of A1 and A2 details; the NBC kit is on both sides, not just the left; there are no CIP panels included; the commander's hatch and SCWS is all wrong ... the list goes on. Sadly, it seems the Trumpeter kits are based on the Heng Long motorised version, which was simply a toy and that it probably the best way to describe Trumpeter's pretty abysmal effort. Tamiya's kit is better. They also produce a radio-controlled version, but the 1/16-scale static display version is basically a scaled-up version of their 1/35-scale kits. If you do feel brave enough to tackle one of the 1/16-scale kits then Special Ops Models has a range of accessories designed for Trumpeter's or Tamiya's kits. The accessories are typical of those that filled the turret stowage racks of M1A1s and M1A2s. These include water and fuel cans, .50cal and 7.62mm ammunition boxes, water coolers, stretcher boards and plastic water bottles.

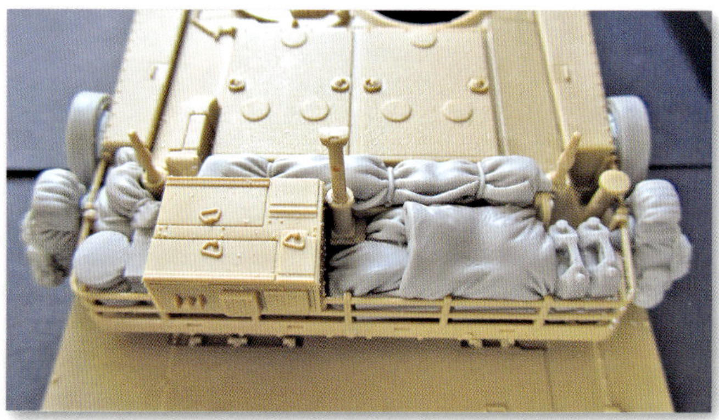

(above) Tetra Model Works and (above right) Red Zebra produce some nice detail and accessories sets for Tamiya's Quarterscale kit.

(below) Trumpeter's 1/16-scale M1A1 has some impressive box art, sadly the contents do not live up to expectations.

(left) Some typically attractive Tamiya box art for their (below) 1/16-scale M1A2.

DETAILING SETS

There is a bewildering array of 1/35-scale detailing kits available for the modeller wanting to improve the appearance of the basic plastic kits of the Abrams Main Battle Tank. This cannot be a comprehensive listing of what is available, but it identifies the major manufacturers and some of the more interesting or unusual items.

Eduard: Czech-firm Eduard are one of the most established names in photoetch detailing, having been in the game for three decades. They are best known for their aircraft detail sets and kits, but the Abrams has not escaped their attention. In 1999 Eduard released sets for the Dragon M1A2 (ref. 35259), the Tamiya M1A1 (ref. 35333) and the Academy M1A1 (ref. 35057). They have released basic detailing set for most new Abrams kits released subsequently, most recently in 2018 for the Panda Model's M1 Abrams (ref. 36381). These sets have some standard parts, some more useful than others. These typically include the bustle rack mesh, replacement ammunition boxes, sprocket ring track retainers where appropriate, and the details for the top of the side skirts, something often missing or poorly represented in most plastic kits. The details suffer of course from the usual 2D nature of photoetch, but on the positive side Eduard sets are among the most user-friendly detailing sets on the market.

Eduard also produce some specific and quite useful detail sets. These include a replacement late-type exhaust cover as used in Iraq for either the Dragon or Tamiya M1A1 (ref. 35600). There is also a bustle rack extension for the Tamiya M1A1 (ref. 35598), as seen on some vehicles during Operation Iraqi Freedom, as well as set of replacement I.F.F./C.I.F. panels for an OIF vehicle (ref. 35594). Eduard have recently slowed their production of armour accessories in favour of aircraft kits and detailing sets and the mantle of premier photoetch details manufacturer now probably rests with two Far

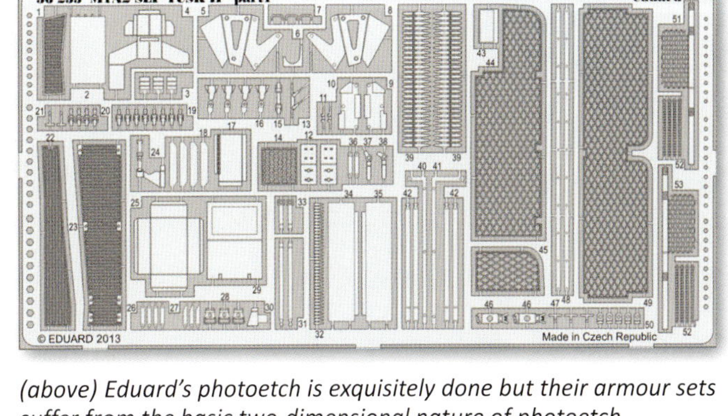

(above) Eduard's photoetch is exquisitely done but their armour sets suffer from the basic two-dimensional nature of photoetch.

(below) Eduard's instructions are very simply drawn and easy to follow.

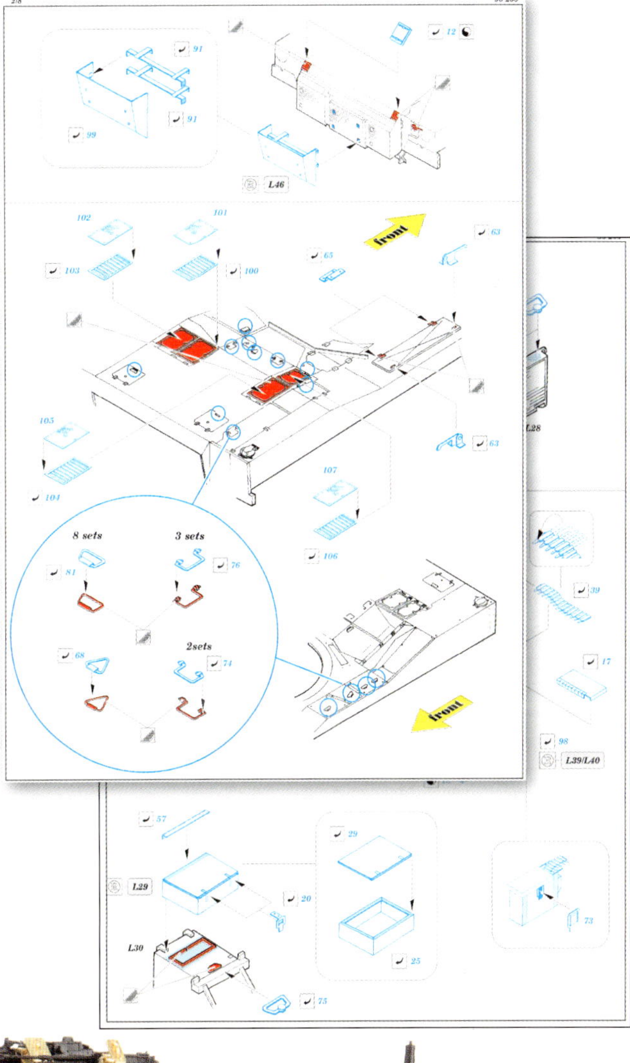

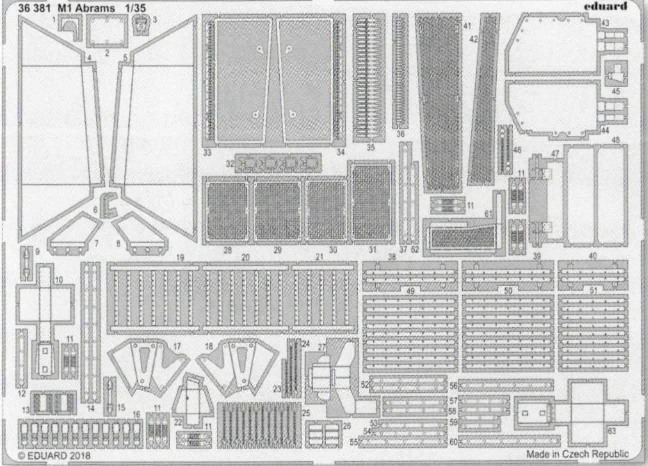

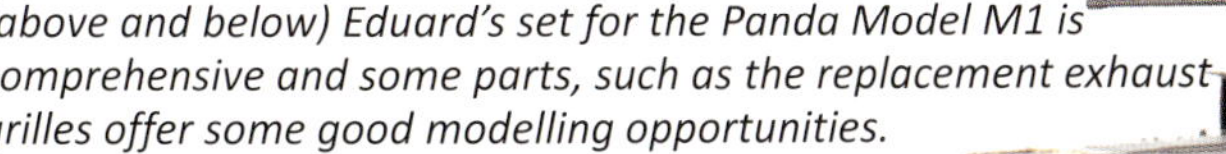

(above and below) Eduard's set for the Panda Model M1 is comprehensive and some parts, such as the replacement exhaust grilles offer some good modelling opportunities.

1-3*. The comprehensive mixed media approach of E.T. Model is evident here.*
4*. Voyager's replacement lenses for the headlights and taillights will lift any Abrams kit.*
5*. PEA148 is Voyager's M1A1/A2 side skirts.*
6*. Voyager's resin gun barrel is a big improvement over any of the kit barrels available.*
7*. The addition of photoetched and resin TUSK parts to Dragon's M1A2 SEP would make for an extraordinary model.*

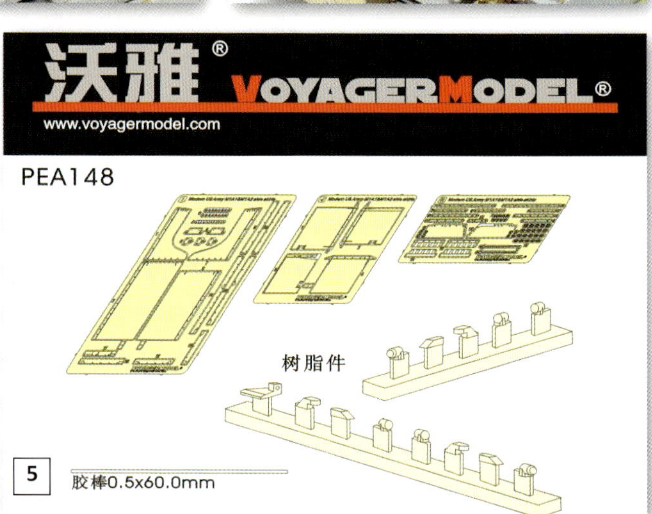

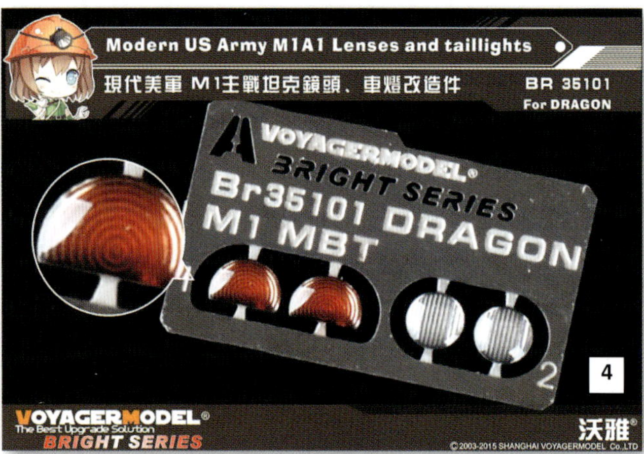

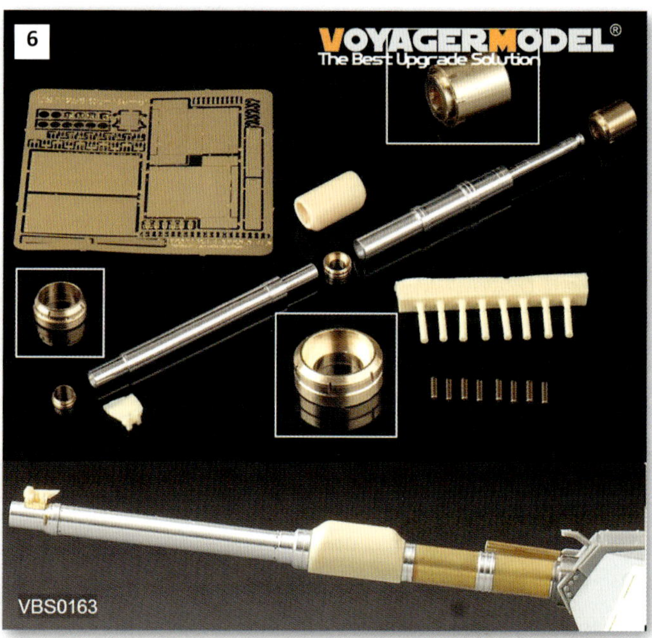

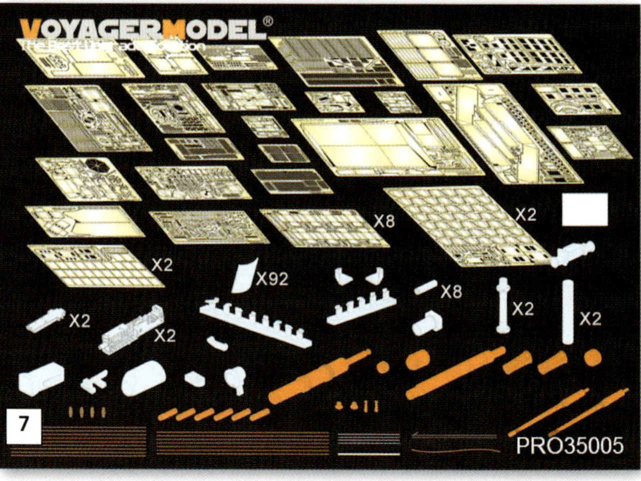

Eastern manufacturers, E.T. Model and Voyager.

E.T. Model: E.T. Model are typical of the new generation of detail set manufacturers. Their sets include photoetched brass, but also resin, turned brass and other media where appropriate. As well as detail sets for the latest generation of Dragon, Meng Model and Tamiya kits, E.T. Model also provide a range of more specific accessory sets. These include a very nice USMC M1A1 MBT Snorkel Set (ref. ER35-052) and an M1A1/A2 Bustle Rack Extension (ref. EA35-042). The E.T. Model sets are not cheap, but they are very extensive. They include photoetch frets of different thickness and such nice accessories as wire antennae bases. You will need some experience and skill in working with photoetch to get the best out of these sets, but care and attention will result in a truly 'superdetailed' model.

Voyager: in a very similar vein to E.T. Model are Voyager Model. Voyager are probably the ultimate in detailing sets and their largest, model kit-specific sets are comprehensive. The set for the M1A2 SEP w/TUSK 2 Pro Kit (ref. PRO35005), designed for the Dragon contains no fewer than 33 sheets of photoetch, over a hundred resin pieces (mainly consisting of 92 M32 ERA tiles), as well as a turned metal M2HB .50cal barrel and multi-part M256 120mm gun barrel. As well as these whole vehicle detailing sets, Voyager offer a range of detail sets that will enhance any Abrams kits: M1A1 lenses and tail lights (ref. BR35101), M1A1 Abrams USMC Snorkel Set (ref. PEA265), a 120mm turned metal and resin gun barrel and smoke dischargers (ref. VBS0163) and the only set of TUSK Slat Armour (ref. PEA149) available in 1/35 scale.

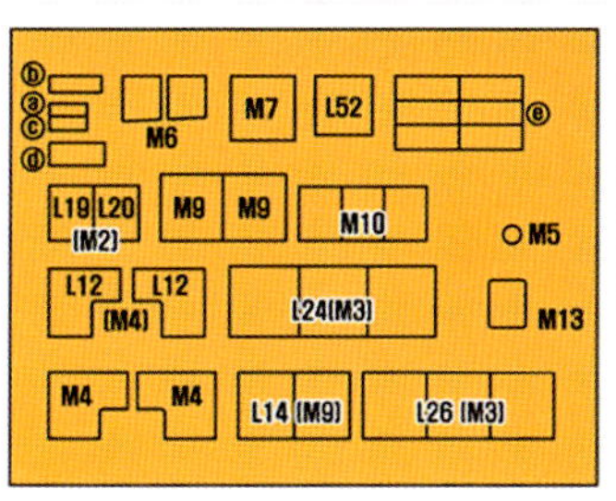

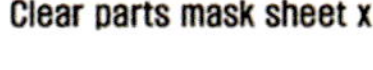

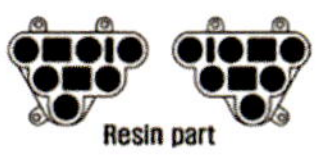

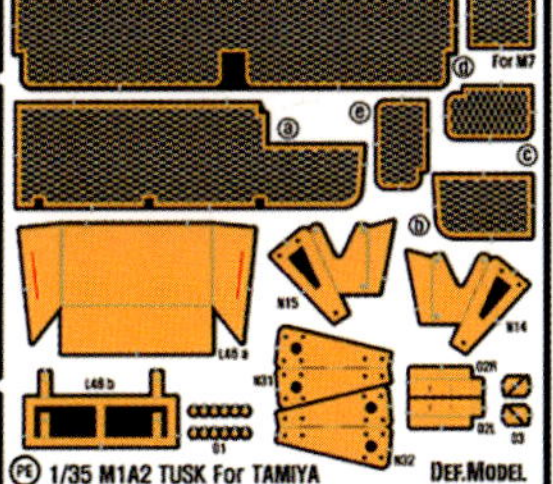

8

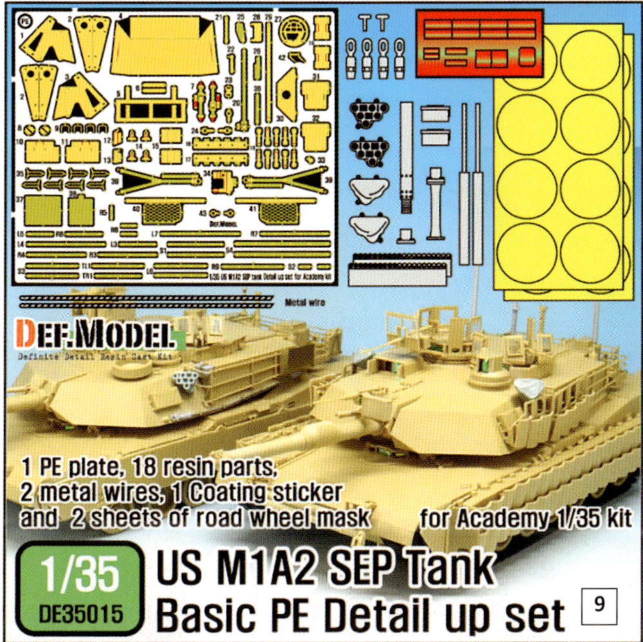

9

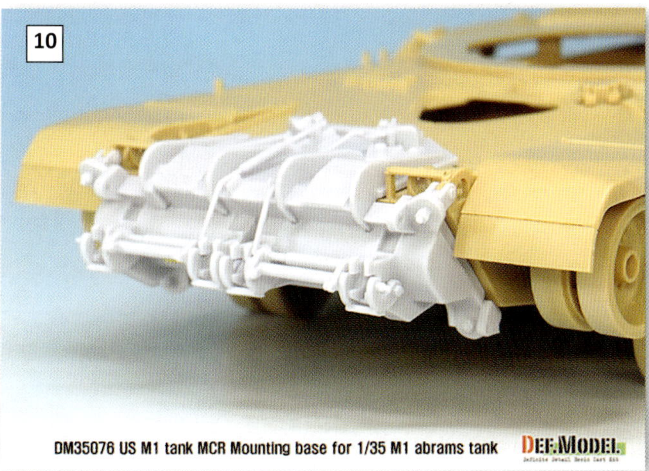

10

8-10. Some of DEF.Models detail and conversion parts.

11. Legend Productions' TUSK conversions are very comprehensive, but as with all resin sets they are not for the inexperienced modeller.

There are several more aftermarket manufacturers that offer accessories and detailing sets in 1/35 scale for the Abrams. These include:

DEF.Model: this South Korean manufacturer is perhaps best known for its range of replacement resin wheels, but they have employed their skills in producing a number of Abrams-related sets. M1A2 SEP TUSK II Basic PE set (ref. DE35006) was released in 2012 and was designed to upgrade the Tamiya kit. As well as photoetched mesh for the smoke discharger mounts and bustle rack mesh, it includes resin smoke dischargers and, best of all, a set of stickers to mimic the distinctive anti-reflection coating seen on the M1A2's vision blocks. DEF.Model have also a detail set for the newer Academy M1A2 (ref. DE35015). This is a really excellent set, including resin tow cable ends, canvas-covered smoke dischargers and new anti-ECM (Electronic Counter Measures) antennae, as well as photoetch, anti-reflective coating stickers and a set of wheel masks to aid painting. In 2014 DEF Model also released a set to convert Dragon's M1A2 SEP to a SEP V2 (ref. DM35030), including a resin CROWS II and other fittings. Perhaps most useful of all, DEF.Model have released an exquisitely designed and cast M1 MCR (Mine Clearing Roller) Mounting Base (ref. DM35076) to fit any of the modern Abrams kits.

Legend Productions: another Korean producer, Legend Productions make a wide range of resin accessories and conversions for 1/35-scale Abrams kits. These fall into two categories: resin conversions for kits (many of these have actually been superseded by new releases) and accessory sets, particularly stowage. Some of the more useful sets include an M1A1 Engine Set (ref. LF1028) and several TUSK I and II conversion sets. These latter have really been superseded by the excellent Academy, Meng Model and Ryefield Model kits though. What are useful though are the various sets of accessories. Legend produce three of these (refs. L1163, LF1177 and LF1359) with the latter being the most comprehensive and including paper MRE cartons and clear plastic water bottles. Be warned though, the large piece of resin stowage covered with a tarpaulin does not fit into the turret bustle stowage rack of the new Academy kit! Legend also produce a 1/48-scale stowage set (ref. LF7207).

Several other manufacturers make accessories sets for Abrams kits. **Orange Hobby** make a couple of resin and turned metal M256 120mm barrels (refs. G35-091-80, G35-113-80, G35-161-98) for the Tamiya, Dragon and Meng Model's kits respectively. These are expensive and difficult to find outside of the Far East. German firm

11

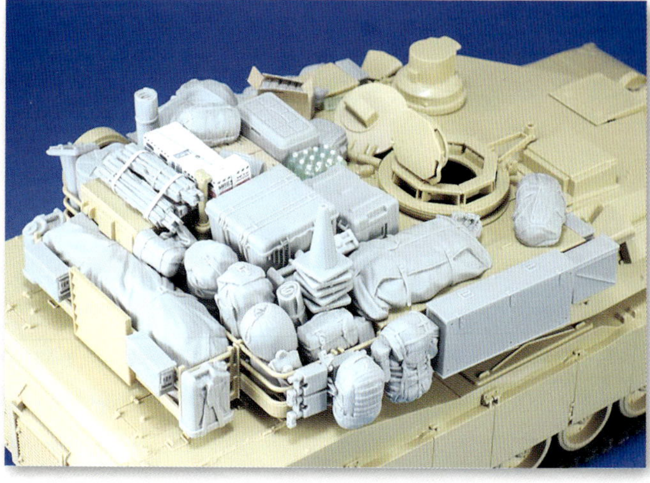

1-2. *Legend Productions' stowage sets are very extensive and beautifully cast.*

3. *One of Orange Hobby's barrel sets.*

4. *As you can see from these instructions, CMK's resin engine set is a pretty comprehensive little kit.*

Perfect Scale Modelbau also offer a couple of TUSK conversions, as well as conversions for USMC M1A1s serving in Iraq and Afghanistan. They also offer a beautifully detailed M1 Dozer Blade (ref. 35101). **CMK** also produce resin M1A2 engines to be dropped into the Dragon and Tamiya kits (refs. 3059, 3138). Photoetched detail sets are offered in both 1/35 and 1/48 scale for the M1A2 by **Tetra Model Works**, while **RB Model** offer an affordable resin and turned metal M256 120mm barrel (ref. 35B106). Japanese firm **Fox Models** also offer some photoetch and resin detail sets, complete with decals. These look excellent, but are expensive and difficult to obtain outside Japan. There are also several detail and conversions sets that are now out of production from the likes of **Real Model** and **Verlinden Productions.** To be honest, many of these have been superseded, but they are worth looking at if you can find them.

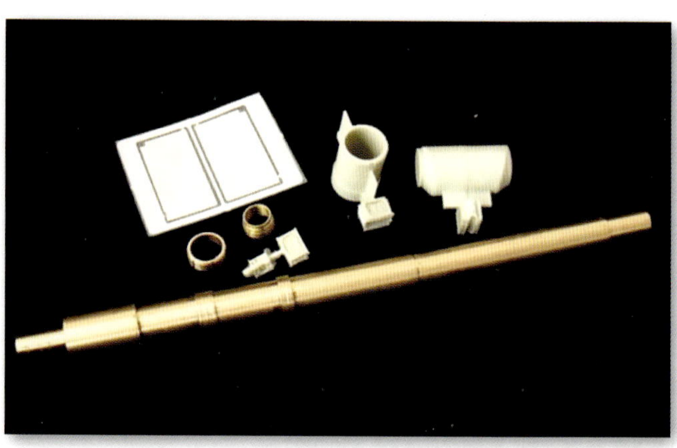

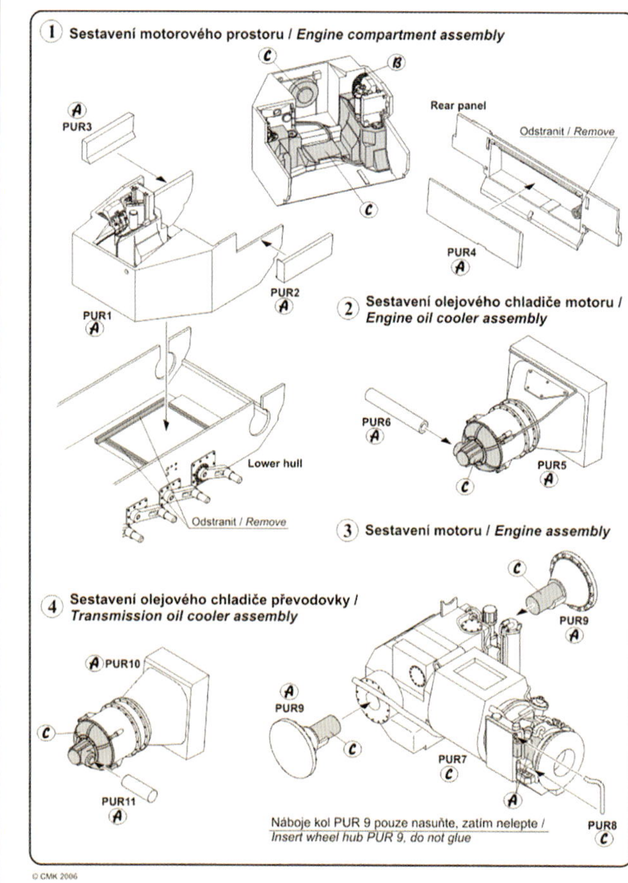

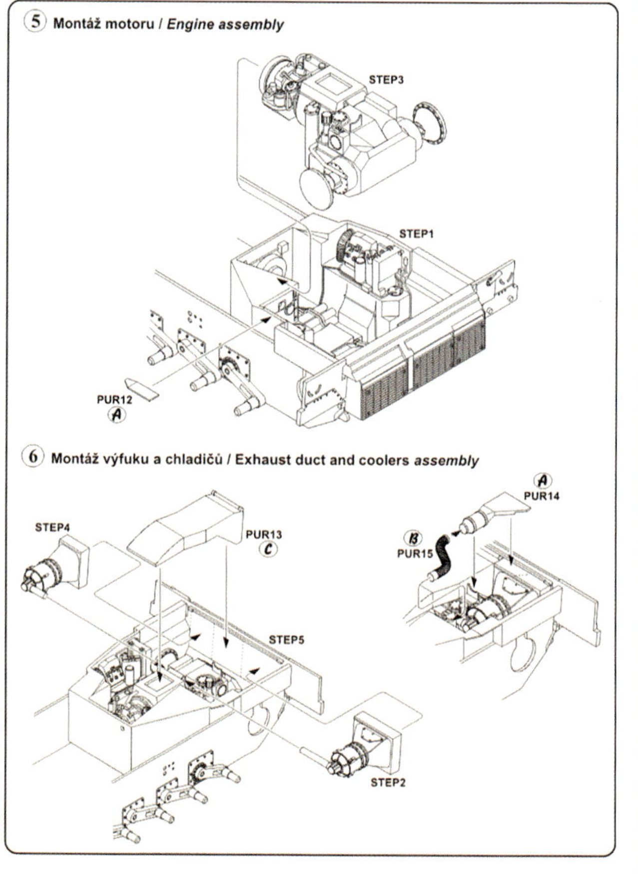

An M1 of 1-11 ACR during Exercise Confident Enterprise in 1983. 11 ACR Abrams wore a makeshift mud camouflage pattern, alongside the prominent Blue Force tactical markings, during REFORGER 83. (NARA: Haggerty Sutherland)

(above) An interesting view of M1s from 1-11 ACR during Exercise Confident Enterprise in 1983. The extremely dark hue of Forest Green, applied to all M1s deployed as part of USAREUR before the adoption of the three-colour NATO scheme, is evident here. (NARA)

Continued from page 14

distinct thawing of US-Soviet relations from the tension-filled years of the early '80s, and in early 1989 a series of popular uprisings and challenges to Soviet-backed government throughout the countries of the Warsaw Pact. This culminated in November with the fall of the Berlin Wall and the symbolic end to the Cold War and the threat of a Soviet invasion of western Europe. This naturally transformed the military imperative and the need to maintain large numbers of US troops and equipment in Germany, although the change did not come overnight. Indeed, as discussions got under way on how to reduce the American presence in Europe, Saddam Hussein invaded Iraq and the world was thrown into a new period of instability. As the first Gulf War ended in the spring of 1991 there were 25 tank battalions, including six cavalry squadrons and two Armored Cavalry Regiments, fielding a total of 1,804 Abrams, based in Germany as part of USAREUR. By 1995 the manpower of USAREUR had been cut from 213,000 in 1990 to 63,000 and the number of tank battalions to just six fielding 402 M1A1s. The Abrams MBTs of USAREUR would continue to see active service, as we shall see, trying to keep peace among the warring parties of the former Yugoslavia, but the tank's days, and its original raison d'être as the West's bulwark against Russian aggression, seemed over.

FIRST GULF WAR

The first combat deployment of the M1 Abrams was far removed from the green fields of the Fulda Gap. In August 1990 Iraq invaded Kuwait. The result was a multinational coalition, led by the United States, stationed in Saudi Arabia to deter future Iraqi aggression and, if diplomatic efforts should fail, to liberate Kuwait by force.

The first US tanks deployed to the Gulf were the forty M551 Sheridans of 82nd Airborne Division, which arrived in Saudi Arabia on 7 August. By the beginning of September, the first M1 Abrams of 24th Infantry Division (Mechanized) had arrived in theatre, followed by 1st Cavalry Division, the 1st 'Tiger' Brigade of 2nd Armored Division and the 3rd Armored Cavalry Regiment. By the end of November 1990 the United States had deployed 760 M1/M1A1 Abrams and 610 M2/M3 Bradley Fighting Vehicles. The build-up of armoured forces continued into the New Year with the arrival of elements of 1st and 3rd Armored Divisions, 2nd Armored Cavalry Regiment, 2nd and 5th Marine Expeditionary Force, the 5th Marine Expeditionary Brigade and various other units. By the time the 15 January deadline for Iraqi forces to leave Kuwait had expired, the United States had deployed nearly 2,000 Abrams (mainly the new 120mm-armed M1A1) and some 300 M60s to Saudi Arabia.

The armour battles of the First Gulf War are well documented and the role of the M1A1s of the US Army have been written about many times before. The Battle of 73 Easting on 26 February 1991, and the battles of Medina Ridge and Norfolk the following day, are synonymous with the absolute superiority of the Coalition forces, both in terms of tactics and equipment. During the so-called Battle of Norfolk, a large action involving US and British armoured forces attempting to cut off the retreat of the Iraqi forces from Kuwait, no fewer than 550 Iraqi tanks and 480 other vehicles were destroyed for the loss of eleven Coalition AFVs. Historians disagree on whether Norfolk was the second largest tank battle ever fought by the US Army (after the Battle of the Bulge), but they can be no doubt that the tank battles of the First Gulf War saw massive deployments of armour not matched by anything since.

A series of lesser-known tank battles during Operation Desert Storm, however, are those fought by Bravo Company of United States Marine Corps' 4th Tank Battalion between 24 and 26 February 1991. These are interesting, not only because of the numerous first-hand accounts which provide a great deal of information on the performance of opposing armour, but also because Bravo Company was a reserve unit and its performance has attracted a certain degree of celebrity. In the aftermath of the Gulf War US media and historians alike celebrated the achievement of the 'farmers, truck drivers, plumbers and college students' who had 'established a combat record unequalled in Marine Corps history'. Although the men of Bravo Company were indeed reservists they were also an elite unit. The company had been activated on 15 December 1990 and arrived at the Marine Corps Air Ground Combat Center at 29 Palms, California, two days later to begin their training on the new M1A1 Abrams. On 2 January 1991 the company begin its gunnery training proper and by

In January 1991 IPM1s and Bradley Fighting Vehicles of 24th Infantry Division prepare for final exercises ahead of the start of ground combat phase of the operation to liberate Kuwait from Saddam Hussein's forces. (NARA: SSgt. F. Lee Corkan)

An M1A1 of 1st Armored Division's 3rd Brigade crosses the northern Kuwaiti desert during Operation Desert Storm. The 3rd Brigade included the Abrams of Taskforces 1-37 Armor and 3-35 Armor and was instrumental in the Allied victory at Medina Ridge. (NARA: SSgt. Robert L. Reeve)

the time they graduated eleven days later they were generally acknowledged as the best company ever to have passed through the training centre.

The company arrived in Saudi Arabia on 21 January and almost immediately had much of their tanks' radios, tools and smoker dischargers pilfered by the regulars Marines of 2nd Tank Battalion! At 04:58 in the morning of 24 February Bravo Company crossed the sand berm and minefields into Kuwait. One M1A1 was lost to a mine but otherwise the company crossed into Kuwait to face the Iraqi armour in good shape. At 16:05 the company was on the left flank of the two mechanized companies of 4th Tank Battalion, both of which reported enemy armour and entrenched infantry to their front. Bravo Company's right flank platoon opened fire on enemy troops in trenches and soon Iraqi soldiers began to emerge from their trenches, hands raised. Bravo Company then surged into an attack, moving over a slight ridge and observing the enemy armour that now threatened the Marine infantry. At ranges from 400 to 3,800 metres, the M1A1 gunners systematically destroyed the out-gunned enemy. This included a BMP-1 destroyed at the amazing range of 3,750 metres and in all the company accounted for ten tanks, fours BMPs, a ZSU 23-4 and sixteen other vehicles. This engagement was called the Battle of the Candy Canes due to the red and white painted towers that ran parallel to the enemy position. The company then withdrew to high ground and 'coiled up' in an overwatch position, its 120mm guns facing outwards.

Early the next morning, 25 February, sentries heard the sound of Soviet-made vehicles to the east of Bravo's coil. The early morning mist and smoke from burning oil fields made identification difficult, but at 05:50 enemy tanks were identified through the thermal sights and the alarm sounded.

Photographed on 24 February 1991, this M1A1 of the USMC's 4th Tank Battalion fitted with a mine plow crosses the sand berm into Kuwait. (NARA: SSgt. Masters)

Another view of two M1A1s of the USMC's 4th Tank Battalion during Operation Desert Storm. Note the brightly coloured aerial identification marker carried by all Coalition forces to prevent 'friendly-fire' incidents. (NARA: SSgt. Masters)

The company began uncoiling to place its 2nd and 3rd platoons on line facing the enemy and 1st platoon on their left slightly refused to the north. An entire Iraqi tank battalion was advancing over a slightly raised hard-surfaced road running north to south approximately 1,800 metres return to the east of Bravo Company's position. Within 90 seconds, most of Bravo Company had engaged the enemy leaving over thirty enemy tanks and personnel carriers in flames. Over the next fifteen minutes, Bravo Company continued to pick off isolated enemy vehicles. Within an hour survivors began to trickle in to Bravo's position. For no casualties themselves, the company destroyed thirty T-72 tanks, four T-55s, and seven APCs. One Abrams commander, Captain Alan Hart, recalled 'When my gunner fired, I saw the round go out and smack a T-72 and blow the turret off.' By the end of the engagement Hart's tank had destroyed seven T-72s in the same fashion with seven rounds of sabot ammunition. The one-sided nature of the engagement was evident to Hart: 'Everything was exploding. Those guys couldn't tell where we were. They had no idea which direction to go. They just knew their vehicles were exploding beneath them.'

On the afternoon of the 25th, Bravo was assigned the base of the battalion's 'V' when the mechanised companies again made contact with Iraqi armour. In increasingly poor visibility, Bravo again took the lead and became engaged with the enemy in a running battle. The enemy was slaughtered at the 'Battle of the L', so-called after L-shaped road junction at which the Marines took up position on the night of 25 February. The battle fought in poor weather and visibility over long hours, but the Abrams still managed to destroy enemy armour at ranges of 2,000 metres while travelling at 20mph! Bravo was credited with the destruction of nine T-62s, twelve BMPs, one MT-LB, three BTR-60s and four trucks. Bravo Company ended its war on the outskirts of Kuwait City, and during four days of combat its thirteen M1A1 Abrams had destroyed 59 Iraqi tanks, including thirty T-72s, and dozens of other vehicles.

Bravo Company's success, which exemplifies the success of US and Coalition armour against the Iraqis in general, was undoubtedly due in part to their own skill and training and the superior gunnery and protection of the M1A1 Abrams. Nevertheless, Iraqi tank tactics were also to blame for the uneven nature of the contest. As Hart recalled: 'I couldn't believe how they came be-bopping across the desert with their guns pointed skywards. They weren't ready to fight us.' Indeed, the Marines were shocked by the lack of communication, training and any sense of tactical awareness the Iraqis demonstrated. As one Marine put it: 'Shit, this is like an NFL team playing a high-school team. These people just didn't understand the operational art of war, they didn't understand cross-boundary fires, they didn't understand fire and manoeuvre. They didn't understand any of the things you need to understand to be successful in combat.'

The 2,000 or so Abrams deployed to the Gulf for Operation Desert Storm were a resounding success. Not a single vehicle was lost entirely to enemy action and it out performed its Soviet-made adversaries – the T-55, T-62 and especially the much-vaunted T-72 – with spectacular effect. The M1's reputation as the most potent main battle tank then in existence was confirmed.

An M1A1 clears mines along the Zone of Separation in Bosnia. This images exemplifies the difficulties of terrain experienced by Abrams crews on peace-keeping missions in the Balkans. (NARA: SSgt. Brian Cumper)

BOSNIA AND KOSOVO

In December 1995 the presidents of Bosnia, Croatia and Serbia signed the Dayton Peace Accords, bringing an end to three-and-a-half years of vicious war in Bosnia. NATO's response was the deployment of IFOR (Implementation Force), a force of some 60,000 personnel organised into three multi-national divisions, to implement the agreement and protect the Bosnian civilian population from Serbian sectarian violence. US forces deployed on 2 December as 'Task Force Eagle' for Operation Joint Endeavour. Under the command of 1st Armored Division, the M1A1s of 1-1 Cavalry, 3-4 Cavalry, 4-67 Armor and 2-68 Armor moved from their bases in Germany by train through Hungary and Croatia to Bosnia. The final leg of the journey was to cross a pontoon bridge spanning the River Sava into Bosnia. As one American officer observed: 'The task force deployed with sufficient force to annihilate the factional armies. Clearly, this was instrumental in ensuring their full cooperation and compliance.'

Task Force Eagle was an armour heavy force, with Swedish, Russian and Turkish AFVs alongside the Abrams of 1st Armored Division. Alongside the M1A1s, Bradley Fighting Vehicles, M113s and M109A6s, there were BTR-80s APCs, BMD-2s, Danish Leopard 1A3s (attached to the Swedish battalion), BV-206S all terrain APCs (much valued by the Americans), Pbv-302s and Finnish SISU XA-180 wheeled APCs. The road network was poorly maintained in Bosnia and the terrain mountainous and difficult for armour. Mud was actually one of the biggest problems faced by the heavy armour of Task Force Eagle and M1A1s were largely restricted to the roads. These were often mined and the mine roller attachments, one of which was issued to each Abrams company, proved invaluable in protecting American personnel and equipment. Most US commanders agreed that the lighter wheeled vehicles and the Russian air-portable BMD-2 were far more effective in actual patrolling and enforcing the Dayton Peace Accords, yet the symbolic presence of the M1A1 was recognised by all the protagonists.

If the NATO intervention in Bosnia was a peace-keeping mission, designed to keep the warring ethnic groups apart and implement a peace settlement, the Alliance faced a much more difficult and dangerous mission three years later in Kosovo. In the summer of 1998 activities by the Kosovo Liberation Army (KLA) led to reprisals by the Yugoslavian and Serbian military, largely aimed against Kosovo's Albanian Muslim population. In October NATO launched limited airstrikes against Yugoslav targets, but the fighting in Kosovo, and the atrocities, intensified. The failure of peace talks led to a much more sustained and intense NATO air campaign, which lasted

M1A1s and crews of Bravo Company, 1-77 Armor during their second rotation as part of Kosovo Force (KFOR) in the summer of 2002. (Ron Mihalko)

An M1A1 of 1-63 Armor on the Falcon 4 Range in Ramnjane, Kosovo, during Operation Joint Guardian. (NARA: Sgt. April Johnson)

from March until June 1999. On 10 June NATO suspended its air campaign when Yugoslavia agreed to withdraw from Kosovo and two days later NATO's Kosovo Force arrived to separate the warring parties and enforce peace in Operation Joint Guardian.

Once again, the M1A1s of 1st Armored Division comprised the main component of the US-led multinational brigade (named Task Force Falcon, continuing the avian theme of the peacekeeping missions in the Balkans), one of five brigades in the NATO force. The tanks of 1-77 Armor arrived in Kosovo on 5 July 1999. The US area of responsibility was the south-east of the country, but the soldiers of Task Force Falcon found themselves in a very different situation from the one that obtained in Bosnia. Although the Serbian security forces had withdrawn, the KLA quickly moved into ethnically mixed areas where violence and reprisals quickly escalated. In their six weeks in theatre the men of 1-77 Armor had to deal with at least eleven murders of ethnic Serbs and over a hundred incidents of violent attacks, looting and arson. Once again, the Abrams proved its worth in a peacekeeping situation: as one officer observed, 'the arrival of M1A1s during a firefight or civil disturbance serves to quiet the situation rather quickly.' The tanks were usually deployed at checkpoints, only occasionally using armoured patrols. The two companies of M1A1s were certainly hampered in their movement by the fragile transport infrastructure of rural south-east Kosovo. While the road system did not prevent the movement of armour, as it had in parts of Bosnia, the damage caused by the M1A1s was not inconsiderable and the utility of tanks had to be weighed against the damage they did in every situation in which they were used. Another problem was the congested and narrow streets, where inquisitive children and nervous tank drivers risked civilian casualties.

The main value of the M1A1 was symbolic, as it had been in Bosnia. As soon as 1-77 Armor arrived, they conducted a 'Thunder Run' to impress on would-be troublemakers that Task Force Falcon meant business: 'How better to protect a facility at risk than to park a 70-ton chariot of destruction next to it?' Yet the M1A1 was not only symbolic in Kosovo; it was also a very potent weapon of war. The ability to engage targets with precision at ranges of up to mile was invaluable, as was the tank's thermal sight in engaging mortar positions. The tankers of 1-77 Armor also found themselves frequently employed as dismounted infantry in Kosovo. This was an unfamiliar role and with only sixteen men in a tank platoon (as opposed to thirty in an infantry one) some improvisation was necessary. The tank platoon only had eight M16 rifles issued and only two men in each crew were fully trained on the M16, so the men of 1-77 Armor were forced to train hard and quickly adapt to the situation in which they found themselves.

The logistical challenges of maintaining 1-77 Armor in the field were not inconsiderable. Prior to deployment, and based on the experience of US armour in Bosnia, considerable time and effort was spent in ensuring the battalion's mine ploughs and rollers were fully mission capable. The M1A1s of 1-77 Armor spent considerable hours in their first two in Kosovo clearing mines and got through no fewer than 350 roadwheels because of the extra burden the mine clearing equipment placed on the Abrams' suspension. 1-77 Armor estimated that the battalion's tanks experienced the equivalent of six months' normal operational wear in their first thirty days in Kosovo.

Over the summer and into the autumn of 1999 the situation in Task Force Eagle's area of operations slowly stabilised. Local arrangements, for example, allowed ethnic Serbian and Albanian farmers from the same village to tend their fields on different days. Such initiatives met with mixed success but the levels of violence did decrease and increasing amounts of Task Force Eagle's efforts were spent dealing with the general lawlessness of the region. On 12 December 1999 the M1A1s of 1-77 Armor were rotated out of Kosovo. In May 2002 1-77 Armor returned to Kosovo as part of KFOR 4A, the fourth rotation of US units there, returning home in November. The lessons learned would be invaluable for American tank crew as their missions continued in the Balkans, but also for what would happen in Iraq in the coming years.

OPERATION IRAQI FREEDOM

The M1 Abrams played a crucial part in the Coalition's victory over the forces of Saddam Hussein as part of Operation Iraqi Freedom in 2003, just as it had done in the First Gulf War twelve years previously. As part of the doctrine of 'Shock and Awe' Abrams from both the US Army and the USMC were at the forefront of the invasion which began on 20 March. On 9 April Baghdad fell after the famous 'Thunder Run', led by Abrams of the 64th Armor Regiment, 3rd Infantry Division. The Abrams proved itself a formidable opponent and a combination of poor training, equipment and tactical employment ensured the Iraqi regular army and Republican Guard were no match for the Coalition armour. Soon after, however, the nature of the conflict changed. Although President Bush had famously proclaimed 'Mission Accomplished' on 1 May 2003, insurgent attacks upon the Coalition forces began to increase leading to the bloody two battles of Fallujah in April and November 2004. By March 2005 some eighty Abrams had been disabled by Iraqi regular forces and insurgents, the vast majority by the latter employing IEDs (Improvised Explosive Devices).

Heavy armour played a crucial role in the US counter-insurgency operation. The Abrams provided both a heavily protected platform, minimising casualties, and an effective means of delivering concentrated, precision firepower on the insurgents. Key developments to the Abrams during this period enabled the tank's successful deployment in Low Intensity Conflict. The new M1028 120 mm anti-personnel canister cartridge contained over a thousand 3⁄8-inch (9.5 mm) tungsten balls, producing a shotgun effect lethal out to 600m. The round was employed both an anti-infantry weapon, but also to destroy concrete buildings. Numerous first-hand accounts of combat in Iraq testify to the effectiveness of the Abrams MBT. A combination of firepower, accuracy, psychological effect, speed and survivability contributed to the tank's battle-winning potential both in the initial invasion and in the anti-insurgency operations that followed. That said, American tank crews frequently found themselves fighting outside their tanks – discarding the old tanker's adage that it's better to die than dismount – and quickly learned that counter-ambush skills and house clearance were vital in surviving combat in Iraq.

The 2nd battalion, 37th Armor Regiment's experience in the holy city of Najaf in April 2004 was typical of the experience of American armoured forces after the heady days of the initial stages of Operation Iraqi Freedom. In April 2004 the radical Shia cleric, Muqtada al-Sadr initiated a nationwide series of uprisings aimed at driving a wedge between Iraq's interim government, the Coalition Forces and Iraq's Shia majority. Al-Sadr's base was in the shrine city of Najaf and its neighbour Kufa, just 150km south of Baghdad. On 22 April Task Force 2-37 Armor, supported by the 2nd and 3rd Armored Cavalry Regiments' diversionary feints along the Euphrates, entered the city of Najaf with a force consisting of 29 M1A1 AIMs, and a large force of HMMWVs and guntrucks. Organised into mixed tank/wheeled vehicle combat teams, the 'Iron Dukes' drew the enemy out in ambushes and then systematically used superior firepower to eliminate the insurgents. By the end of May al-Sadr's

US Marine Corps personnel from Charlie Company, USMC 1st Tank Battalion, sit on their M1A1s in an assembly area near Az Zubayr, Iraq two days into Operation Iraqi Freedom. (NARA: Sgt. Paul L. Anstine II)

forces were isolated in the old town of Najaf, but remained in strength in nearby Kufa. On 30 May TF 2-37 Armor, consisting of three company-strength tank forces from the Iron Dukes as well as from the 2nd and 3rd Armored Cavalry Regiments, initiated Operation Smackdown, designed to destroy the militia in Kufa and force al-Sadr into a political settlement. By 3 June the Abrams of TF 2-37 Armor had fought to Kufa Mosque, destroying insurgent weapons caches and eliminating an estimated 1,000 enemy fighters.

The fighting in Najaf and Kufa demonstrated the effectiveness of the Abrams as part of a combined arms teams (which crucially also involved Coalition airpower, especially attack helicopters) in a complex and rapidly shifting battlefield. One of the key considerations for US commanders was the need to avoid collateral damage; a 120mm shell hole in the dome of the Iman Ali shrine would have done incalculable damage to the Coalition efforts to defeat the insurgency. Lieutenant Colonel Pat White, commander of TF 2-37 Armor, observed: 'The most precise weapons system in the task force was the M1A1 main battle tank. The coaxial-mounted M240 machine gun is precision at its best...The tank also has the most accurate and deadly system available — the 120mm main gun. Tank commanders learned early on that firing a multipurpose antitank (MPAT) round, a high-explosive antitank (HEAT) round, or an obstacle-reducing (OR) round immediately silenced enemy massed formations due to tremendous psychological effects. A tank can fire a main gun round through a window and destroy the enemy while damaging only one room, minimizing collateral damage. Tanks can also create entry points for scouts or infantry by firing a main gun round into the wall of a school or directly into the side of a building. OR and MPAT rounds are effective in destroying hasty obstacles, and the task force even used the MPAT round to suppress enemy dismounts on the street.

The task force relied on the main gun after experiencing the effects of the tank commander's .50-calibre in close urban terrain. Armour-piercing incendiary (API) .50-calibre rounds are devastating and

(above) A sketch drawn in April 2003 by USMC Sgt. Jack M. Carrillo showing an M1A1 gunner from 1st Tank Battalion in during Operation Iraqi Freedom. (NARA)

(below) M1A1s from Charlie Company, USMC 1st Tank Battalion roll along Highway 27 near An Nu'maniyah, Iraq, during the opening stages of Operation Iraqi Freedom in April 2003. (NARA: Sgt. Paul L. Anstine II)

An M1A1 of Task Force 1-35 Armor, 2nd Brigade Combat Team, 1st Armored Division patrols through Baghdad in November 2003. (NARA: TSgt John L. Houghton Jr)

accurate, but cause a significant amount of collateral damage. The API round will pass through four to five buildings without slowing down. The round demolishes concrete structures and sets flammable materials, such as palm and date trees ablaze. During one fight, an RPG gunner was hiding behind an Alaska barrier, which is concrete, reinforced with rebar, and twelve feet high, and instead of using a main gun round, he shot fifty rounds of API into the base of the Alaska barrier, killing the RPG gunner and clearing the area.'

The USMC founds its Abrams MBTs equally invaluable during the second battle for Fallujah in November 2004. The

A USMC M1A1 Abrams from 1st Tank Battalion moves into position during a USMC mortar counter-battery fire attack against Iraqi insurgents in Fallujah in April 2004. (NARA: LCpl Jordan F. Sherwood)

(above) A USMC M1A1 in Fallujah during Operation Al Fajr (Phantom Fury) in November 2004. The battered appearance of the tank is testimony to the heavy street fighting in which the Marines' Abrams took the lead. (NARA: LCpl Benjamin J. Flores)

(below) A M1A1 Abrams tank, from Bravo Company, 1-35 Armor, 2nd Brigade Combat Team, 1st Armored Division in Iraq in December 2008. Note the TUSK 1 kit fitted to improve survivability in an urban combat environment. (US Army: Chase Kincaid)

lessons learned in Najaf and Kufa were replicated during Operation Phantom Fury. In the opening stages of the battle for Fallujah a company of M1A1s fought alongside the 3-1st and 3-5th Marines. Tanks, the Marines reported, were the weapon of choice against enemy in strong points, precisely because they were able to minimise collateral damage. They also proved extremely resilient: the company commander's M1A1, for instance, was hit seven times by RPGs in one day and only needed minor repairs before re-entering the battle. Nevertheless, the USMC armour was not sufficient and the Marines called upon the Army's 2-7 Cavalry for support. Their different tactics, however, caused some friction. An after-action report complained that the Army were reluctant to commit their tanks to the business of house clearing. The commander of Charlie Company, 2nd Tank Battalion observed: 'My tanks were the ones that did the detailed clearing with [the Marine infantry] for over two months. As for survivability, I would say our M1A1s are better in that area. The .50 cal machine gun proved to be vital in our fight, the M1A2 SEP tank when buttoned up (as they were the whole time) completely precludes the use of their [cupola-mounted] .50cal.'

The experiences in Fallujah and elsewhere had proved the tank's worth in urban combat, a situation quite different from the plains of central Europe which the designers of the M1 had envisaged would be their tank's principal theatre of operations. The experience of war in Iraq led to the development of the TUSK (Tank Urban Survival Kit), a series of field-installed Reactive Armour tiles, passive armour belly protection, and (initially at least) slat armour designed to counter IEDs, RPGs and other insurgent tactics. The kit also included enhanced protection for the commander and loader, allowing them to observe the battlefield behind armoured glass and a second coaxial 12.7mm M2HB machine gun mounted directly above the main gun and fired remotely. By 2008 550 TUSK packages had been delivered and they proved successful in Iraq improving the survivability of the tank and saving the lives of many Abrams crewmen.

M1A1s of 1st Tank Battalion, USMC, refuel near Jalibah Airfield, Iraq, on 24 March 2003. (NARA: Sgt. Paul L. Anstine II)

A destroyed M1A1 of 2nd Tank Battalion, USMC, near Sayyid Abd, Iraq, in April 2003 during Operation Iraqi Freedom. (NARA: MSgt. Howard J. Farrell

An M1A2 SEP of 1-66 Armor pauses as they protect Shi'ite pilgrims en route to the Karbala shrine in Iraq in March 2006. (NARA: Katrina Beeler)

ABRAMS TODAY

The end of the Cold War and the subsequent reconfiguration of the US Armed Forces to fight 'The War on Terror' led to a questioning of the need for MBTs among the political and military establishment in Washington. In a world of budgetary constraints following the 2009 Financial Crisis and where it was believed in some circles that the fundamental nature of warfare had changed, a school of thought argued that the MBT was redundant and that wars in the future would be waged through UAVs (Unmanned Aerial Vehicles), long-range ballistic ordnance, special forces and an increased use of electronic warfare. The last remaining US armoured units were withdrawn from Germany in 2013 and the Department of Defense planned to end production of the Abrams MBTs at the Lima Army Tank Plant from 2013 to 2016. The Ukrainian crisis of 2014 and the Russian annexation of Crimea, however, changed the geopolitical situation and forced the United States to reassess its warfighting capabilities. Concern among the United States' northern and central European NATO partners led to Operation Atlantic Resolve, an American-led NATO effort to assure Russia's nearest neighbours, and particularly the Baltic States, of NATO's continuing commitment to their defence. From 2015, as part of the European Reassurance Initiative, until its redeployment to the United States in September 2017, the 3rd Armored Brigade Combat Team of the 4th Infantry Division, with its 87 M1A2 Abrams, was stationed in Germany to demonstrate the United States' commitment to European security. The unit took part in well-publicised NATO exercises from Estonia to Bulgaria. These exercises marked a renewed emphasis on Combined Arms Manoeuvre and tactical co-operation between NATO partners as part of a wider reorientation of the mission of the US armoured force to face a peer or near-peer adversary in the future. This new environment was greeted with some trepidation and not a little panic in some quarters of the American military. In 2017 President Trump's new National Security Advisor Lt. Gen. H.R. McMaster, himself an experienced and decorated Abrams commander, observed that the 'Russians have superior artillery firepower, better combat vehicles ... should US forces find themselves in a land war with Russia, they would be in for a rude, cold awakening.'

The US Army's Abrams are currently deployed across ten Armored Brigade Combat Teams (ABCT), with a further five National Guard ABCTs. Each ABCT has a nominal strength of 90 tanks and contain two armoured battalions (two tank companies and a mechanized infantry company) and two mechanized infantry battalions (one tank company and two mechanized infantry companies). Currently two versions of the Abrams are fielded by the US Army: the M1A2 SEP V2 and the M1A1 SA (in service with National Guard units).

One of the key challenges facing the US Army's Armored Brigade Combat Teams in this new environment is to improve lethality; in other words, to improve the effectiveness of gunnery and interoperability with other arms to decisively defeat a peer opponent in, as General Mark Miller, the Chief of the Staff of the Army, terms it, 'the unforgiving crucible of ground combat'. To this end the US Army's Abrams have all been upgraded to M1A2 SEP V2 standard and the number of Live Fire Exercises, both at the National Training Center at Fort Irwin, CA, and in Europe, has increased. The aim of this is to recreate battlefield experience among junior commanders in the Armored Brigade Combat Team, allowing them to make the right tactical decisions to maximise lethality. Another problem recently identified is the departure and rotation of experienced Abrams crews from the Armored Brigade Combat Teams.

Another important moment in this transition from Low Intensity Combat (LIC) of the kind encountered in Iraq to preparation for the kind of peer-on-peer encounter that dominated Cold War military planning was

An M88A2 Hercules recovery vehicle, of 3-69 Armor, 1st Armored Brigade Combat Team, 3rd Infantry Division tows a M1A2 SEP V2 during exercise Combined Resolve IV at the US Army's Joint Multinational Readiness Center in Hohenfels, Germany in May 2015. (US Army: Spc. Tyler Kingsbury)

An M1A2 SEP V2 from 1-8 Cavalry, 2nd Armored Brigade Combat Team, 1st Cavalry Division conducts a situational training exercise (STX) in Dagmar, South Korea in November 2017. The United States maintains one Armored Brigade Combat Team permanently in South Korea as part of their commitment to the defence of the peninsula. (US Army: Sgt Patrick Eakin)

the Tactical Road March carried by the 2nd Armored Brigade Combat Team, 'the Dagger Brigade', of 1st Armored Division on 22 and 23 April 2018. This was the first brigade-strength tactical road march to take place since the end of the Cold War and was part of Combined Resolve X, a multi-national exercise involving 3,700 participants from thirteen Allied and partner nations. 2nd Armored Brigade Combat Team transported some 850 vehicles along approximately 60km of German public roads between the two training centres at Grafenwoehr to Hohenfels in Bavaria in no fewer than 22 separate convoys. This concentration of armour certainly attracted a huge amount of attention from the press and from the civilian population and highlighted the central role that the Abrams Main Battle Tank plays in the United States' warfighting capability.

UNITED STATES MARINE CORPS

In 2004, following the completion of the initial stages of Operation Iraqi Freedom, the Marine Corps Force Structure Review Board approved the reduction of the USMC's tank force from four regular and one reserve battalions to just three (one a reserve) battalions. The USMC currently has some 120 M1A1s in service. The role of the Marine Corps' Abrams remains to close with and destroy the enemy using expeditionary armour-protected firepower, shock effect, and manoeuvre in support of the MAGTF (Marine Air-Ground Task Forces) across the range of military operations. The two active battalions currently serve as part

An M1A2 SEP V2 of 1-63 Armor, 2nd Armored Brigade Combat Team, 1st Infantry Division, conducts a live-fire exercise on the range at Grafenwoehr, Germany, in April 2018.

The worn coat of RAL6031 paint over the usual CARC Tan was typical of US AFVs in Europe in 2016-18 (US Army: Spc. Genesis Gomez)

(above) An M1A2 SEP V2 of 2nd Armored Brigade Combat Team during the tactical road march from Grafenwoehr Training Area, Germany to Hohenfels during Combined Resolve X on 23 April 2018. (US Army: Spc. Dustin D. Biven)

(below) An M1A2 SEP V3 of 2-34 Armor, 1st Armored Brigade Combat Team, fitted with a mine clearance plow, during Exercise Allied Spirit X at the Hohenfels Training Centre in April 2019. (US Army: SPC Malik Johnson)

(bottom) An M1A1 of Delta Company, 1st Tank Battalion, Regimental Combat Team 7, at Camp Shir Ghazay, Helmand Province, Afghanistan, in April 2013. (US Marine Corps: Staff Sgt. Ezekiel R. Kitandwe)

of the I and II Marine Expeditionary Forces, based at Camp Pendleton, CA, and Camp Lejeune, NC, respectively.

The USMC's M1A1s were last deployed on active service as part of NATO's operation in Hellmand and Kandahar provinces, Afghanistan. In late 2010 fourteen M1A1s of Delta Company, 1st Tank Battalion were deployed to southern Afghanistan. The company remained in theatre for six months before being replaced by the battalion's other companies on rotation until July 2013. The USMC also deployed the M1 Assault Breacher Vehicle to Afghanistan alongside its M1A1. Today the USMC's Abrams and their crews face the same challenges as their Army counterparts in making the transition to preparing for peer-to-peer combat. In 2018 and 2019 the M1A1s of the USMC have been deployed on live-fire exercises in the Baltic and Scandinavia as part of NATO manoeuvres and in Exercise Cobra Gold involving US, Thai, South Korean, Japanese, Malaysian, Singaporean and Indonesian forces, as well as those of India and China.

(above) An M1A1 of 2nd Tank Battalion, 2nd Marine Division practises crossing an expeditionary bridge during Exercise Trident Juncture in Norway, October 2018. (US Marine Corps: 2nd Lt. Larry Boyd Jr)

(below) An M1A1 of Charlie Company, 4th Tank Battalion fires during Exercise Cobra Gold 19 at Sukhothai, Kingdom of Thailand in February 2019. (US Marine Corps: Sgt. Kyle C. Talbot)

A rather battered looking M1A2 SEP V2 of 1-68 Armor, 3rd Armored Brigade Combat Team, 4th Infantry Division, during a Combined Arms Live Fire exercise at the 7th Army Training Command's Grafenwoehr Training Area, Germany, in July 2017. (US Army: Visual Information Specialist Gertrud Zach)

An M1A2 SEP V2 of 1-63 Armor, 2nd Armored Brigade Combat Team, 1st Infantry Division, during Exercise Combined Resolve at Hohenfels Training Area, Germany, in May 2018. Note the M1 Mine Clearing Roller attachment on the hull front. (US Army: Spc. Andrew McNeil)

A good view of the distinctive Stabilised Commander's Weapon System fitted to a M1A1 FEP of the 2nd Tank Battalion of the 26th Marine Expeditionary Unit during NATO Baltic Operations (BALTOPS) exercise in June 2018. (USMC: Staff Sgt. Dengrier M. Baez)

THE M1 IN FOREIGN SERVICE

Currently, the M1 Abrams serves in the armed forces of six other nations: Australia, Egypt, Iraq, Kuwait, Morocco and Saudi Arabia.

Australia: in 2006 Australia bought 59 M1A1 AIM SA (Situational Awareness) tanks (without the depleted uranium armour) to replace its Leopard AS1 fleet. There is close cooperation between the Australian and US armoured units and a team from Australia (as well as one from Kuwait) competed against American tank crews in the 2018 annual Sullivan Cup. The Australian government has approved an upgrade to its Abrams fleet to M1A2 SEP V2 standard, which may also involve an expansion of the number of Abrams in its inventory.

Egypt: Egypt has assembled M1A1 tanks in Egypt since 1988 and by 2010 had completed over 1,000 vehicles. In 2011 the tanks were deployed to the streets of Cairo during the popular uprising against the government of Hosni Mubarak. US cooperation was withdrawn following the military coup of 2013, but restored two years later and the Egyptian Abrams fleet is projected to reach 1,130.

Iraq: in 2011 the United States delivered 146 M1A1 SA tanks to Iraq with a view to further deliveries in subsequent years. In 2014 the Iraqi Abrams were deployed against ISIS with disastrous results: within three months roughly a third had been damaged, captured or destroyed by the militants. By the end of the year only about 40 Abrams remained serviceable with the Iraqi army. Several of the captured tanks were employed by Da'ish (or ISIS) and also found their way into the hands of other militant groups in Iraq and Syria and at least one has been seen operating under the flag of Hizbollah in Syria. The United States has refused to supply further tanks to Iraq and the Iraqi army has recently taken delivery of T-90S tanks from Russia. In the future Iraq plans to operate two armoured brigades, one equipped with Abrams, the other with T-90s!

Kuwait: in 1993, in the wake of the First Gulf War, Kuwait purchased 218 M1A2s which remain in service today.

(top) An Egyptian M1A1 in the streets of Cairo during the 2011 revolution. Note how graffiti daubed on the side skirts by protestors has been scrubbed off by its crew. (Essam Sharaf)

(above) An Iraqi M1A1 gets into position during tactical training with Iraqi infantry soldiers at Camp Taji, Iraq, in March 2015 in preparation for their deployment to northern Iraq to fight Da'ish. (US Air Force: Senior Airman James Richardson)

Morocco: in 2015 Morocco ordered 222 M1A1s refurbished to SA standard. The first delivery took place in July 2016 with a further one in April this year. The latter caused something of a stir when photos of a train carrying the tanks from the Lima Tank Factory attracted the attention of conspiracy theorists on Social Media!

Saudi Arabia: the Saudis purchased 315 M1A2s in 1993. In 2008, at a cost of almost $3 billion, the fleet was upgraded to M1A2S (basically SEP specifications without the depleted uranium armour). The Saudi M1s have seen action in Yemen recently against the Houthi rebels, where at least twenty have been lost to enemy action since 2015, mainly to ATGMs (anti-tank guided missiles).

AUSSIE ABRAMS

Until the end of 2017 most of the M1A1s of the Royal Australian Armoured Corps served in the 1st Armoured Regiment, based in Darwin. The regiment consisted of three sabre squadrons of fourteen tanks each and two with the regimental HQ. In November 2017 the RAAC reorganised so that one squadron of M1A1s now serves in each of the three armoured regiments: 1st Armoured Regiment in Adelaide, 2nd Cavalry Regiment in Townsville and 2nd/14th Light Horse Regiment (Queensland Mounted Infantry) in Brisbane.

(right) Alongside its M1A1s, the RAAC also acquired seven M88A2 HERCULES Heavy Armoured Recovery Vehicles. This one was photographed during Exercise Hamel in 2016, a joint Australian/USMC training event held at the Cultana Training Area, South Australia. (US Marine Corp: Cpl. Mandaline Hatch)

(top, bottom) M1A1s of the 1st Armoured Regiment at the Cambrai Day celebrations on 20 November 2017. The event, at RAAF Base Edinburgh, marked the arrival of the regiment to their new barracks in South Australia. The photos show the pattern of the distinctive AusCam colour scheme – Tan, Green and Black – introduced in 2010. (David Harvey)

1st Armoured Regiment M1A1s at the Shoalwater Bay Military Training Centre in Queensland in 2013. As you can see, Aussie Abrams take quite a battering in harsh environment of the Queensland Bush. (David Harvey)

Further Reading

The definitive account of the development and early history of the M1 remains R.P. Hunnicitt, *Abrams: A History of the American Main Battle Tank, Volume 2* (1990, repr. 2015)

Steve Zaloga's three volumes for Osprey Publishing are good starting points: *The M1 Abrams Battle Tank* (Vanguard 41), *M1 Abrams Main Battle Tank 1982-1992* (New Vanguard 2), *M1A2 Abrams Main Battle Tank 1993-2018* (New Vanguard 268)

Also worth looking at are:

Michael Green and Greg Stewart, *M1 Abrams at War* (2005)

M1 Abrams Main Battle Tank From 1980 (M1, M1A1 and M1A2 Models) (Haynes Owners' Workshop Manual)

David Doyle, *Images of War: M1 Abrams* (2019) has some very useful walkarounds of museum vehicles

Armor magazine, the publication of the US Army's Armor School at Fort Benning, GA, is invaluable for first-hand accounts of the Abrams in service. Issues from 1983 to the present can be downloaded at www.dvids.com.

There are several excellent photo albums which will serve as inspiration for any modeller planning an Abrams project. These include:

Yves Debay, M1 Abrams (Histoire & Collections, 2006)

M1-M1 IP-M1A1 Abrams Main Battle Tank (Verlinden Warmachines 6)

There are several Tankograd volumes that cover the Abrams in particular or as part of their coverage of military exercises. Notable among these are:

Walter Böhm, *Cold War Warrior: M1/IPM1 Abrams* (Tankograd American Special 3023)

Carl Schulze, *M1A1/M1A2 SEP Abrams TUSK* (Tankograd American Special 3009)

Gordon Arthur, *Australian M1A1 Abrams* (International Special 8008)

Some of the best photo albums on the Abrams are produced by Sabot Publications.

M1A2 Main Battle Tank, Volume 2 (SP005, 2016)

M1A1 Main Battle Tank, Volume 1: Iraq (SP006, 2017)

M1A2 Main Battle Tank (SP007, 2017)

M1 ABV Assault Breacher Vehicle (Warmachines Photo Reference Book 01)

M1A2 in Europe (Warmachines Photo Reference Book 03)

M1A1 SA in Iraqi Service (Warmachines Photo Reference Book 04)

My thanks to Mark Smith, MP Robinson, Carl Schulze, Ron Mihalko, David Harvey, Chris Jerrett, Mark Chisholm, John Murphy, Artur Walachowski, Joaquin Garcia Gazquez and Vorya Heidaryan for their help in contributing ideas, photographs and models for this volume. This volume could also not have been written without the resources of the National Archives and Records Administration and the Defense Visual information Distribution Service (DVIDS).

An M1A2 SEP V2 powers through the smoke during the 2018 Strong Europe Tank Challenge. (US Army: Matthis Fruth)